volume 4 20 Presentations for Spring

the complete guide to
Godly Play

Jerome W. Berryman

An imaginative method for presenting scripture stories to children

TABLE OF CONTENTS

INTRODUCTION

Welcome to *The Complete Guide to Godly Play, Volume 4.* In this volume, we gather together the presentations that form the suggested cycle of lessons for Spring. *Volume 1* of the series, *How to Lead Godly Play Lessons*, provides an in-depth overview of the process and methods of Godly Play. Below, you'll find only quick reminder notes. Please refer to *Volume 1* for an in-depth presentation.

Following this Introduction, you'll find all the information you need to present the lessons of Spring to the children in your Godly Play room. We hope the simple format will enable all teachers, whether new or experienced, to find the information they need to enter fully into the most rewarding play we share: Godly Play.

WHAT IS GODLY PLAY?

Godly Play is what Jerome Berryman calls his interpretation of Montessori religious education. It is an imaginative approach to working with children, an approach that supports, challenges, nourishes and guides their spiritual quest. It is more akin to spiritual direction than to what we generally think of as religious education.

Godly Play assumes that children have some experience of the mystery of the presence of God in their lives, but that they lack the language, permission and understanding to express and enjoy that in our culture. In Godly Play, we enter into parables, silence, sacred stories and sacred liturgy in order to discover God, ourselves, one another and the world around us.

In Godly Play, we prepare a special environment for children to work with adult guides. Two teachers guide the session, making time for the children:
• to enter the space and be greeted
• to get ready for the presentation
• to enter into a presentation based on a parable, sacred story or liturgical action
• to respond to the presentation through shared wondering
• to respond to the presentation (or other significant spiritual issue) with their own work, either expressive art or with the lesson materials
• to prepare and share a feast
• to say goodbye and leave the space

To help understand what Godly Play *is*, we can also take a look at what Godly Play is *not*. First, Godly Play is *not* a complete children's program. Christmas pageants, vacation Bible schools, children's choirs, children's and youth groups, parent-child retreats, picnics, service opportunities and other components of a full and vibrant children's ministry are all important and are not in competition with Godly Play. What Godly Play contributes to the glorious mix of activities is the heart of the matter, the art of knowing and knowing how to use the language of the Christian people to make meaning about life and death.

Godly Play is different from many other approaches to children's work with scripture. One popular approach is having fun with scripture. That's an approach we might find in many church school pageants, vacation Bible schools or other such suggested children's activities.

Having superficial fun with scripture is fine, but children also need deeply *respectful* experiences with scripture if they are to fully enter into its power. If we leave out the heart of the matter, we risk trivializing the Christian way of life. We also miss the profound fun of existential discovery, a kind of "fun" that keeps us truly alive!

HOW DO YOU DO GODLY PLAY?

When doing Godly Play, *be patient*. With time, your own teaching style, informed by the practices of Godly Play, will emerge. Even if you use another curriculum for church school, you can begin to incorporate aspects of Godly Play into your practice —beginning with elements as simple as the greeting and goodbye.

Pay careful attention to the environment you provide for children. The Godly Play environment is an "open" environment in the sense that children may make genuine choices regarding both the materials they use and the process by which they work toward shared goals. The Godly Play environment is a "boundaried" environment in the sense that children are protected and guided to make constructive choices.

As teachers, we set nurturing boundaries for the Godly Play environment by managing *time, space* and *relationships* in a clear and firm way. The setting needs such limits to be the kind of safe place in which a creative encounter with God can flourish. Let's explore each of these in greater depth.

HOW TO MANAGE TIME

AN IDEAL SESSION

In its research setting, a full Godly Play session takes about two hours. An ideal session has four parts, each part echoing the way most Christians organize their worship together.

OPENING: ENTERING THE SPACE AND BUILDING THE CIRCLE

The storyteller sits in the circle, waiting for the children to enter. The door person helps children and parents separate outside the room, and helps the children slow down as they enter the room. The storyteller helps each child sit in a specific place in the circle, and greets each child warmly by name.

The storyteller, by modeling and direct instruction, helps the children get ready for the day's presentation.

HEARING THE WORD OF GOD: PRESENTATION AND RESPONSE

The storyteller first invites a child to move the hand of the Church "clock" wall hanging to the next block of color. The storyteller then presents the day's lesson. At the presentation's end, the storyteller invites the children to wonder together about the lesson. The storyteller then goes around the circle asking each child to choose work for the day. If necessary, the door person helps children get out their work, either storytelling materials or art supplies. As the children work, some might remain with the storyteller who presents another lesson to them. This smaller group is made up of those who aren't able to choose work on their own yet.

SHARING THE FEAST: PREPARING THE FEAST AND SHARING IT IN HOLY LEISURE

The door person helps three children set out the feast—such as juice, fruit or cookies—for the children to share. Children take turns saying prayers, whether silently or aloud, until the last prayer is said by the storyteller. The children and storyteller share the feast, then clean things up and put the waste in the trash.

DISMISSAL: SAYING GOODBYE AND LEAVING THE SPACE

The children get ready to say goodbye. The door person calls each child by name to say goodbye to the storyteller. The storyteller holds out hands, letting the child make the decision to hug, hold hands or not touch at all. The storyteller says goodbye and reflects on the pleasure of having the child in this community.

In the research setting, the opening, presentation of the lesson and wondering aloud together about the lesson might take about half an hour. The children's response to the lesson through art, retelling and other work might take about an hour. The preparation for the feast, the feast and saying goodbye might take another half an hour.

IF YOU ONLY HAVE THE FAMOUS FORTY-FIVE MINUTE HOUR

You may have a limited time for your sessions—as little as forty-five minutes instead of two hours. With a forty-five-minute session, you have several choices.

FOCUS ON THE FEAST

Sometimes children take especially long to get ready. If you need a full fifteen minutes to build the circle, you can move directly to the feast, leaving time for a leisurely goodbye. You will not shortchange the children. The *quality* of time and relationships that the children experience within the space *is* the most important lesson presented in a session of Godly Play.

FOCUS ON THE WORD

Most often, you will have time for a single presentation, including time for the children and you to respond to the lesson by wondering together. Finish with the feast and then the goodbye ritual. Because the children will have no time to make a work response, we suggest that every three or four sessions, you omit any presentation and focus on the work instead (see directly below).

FOCUS ON THE WORK

If you usually must pass from the presentation directly to the feast, then every three or four sessions, substitute a work session for a presentation. First build the circle. Then, without making a presentation, help children choose their work for the day. Allow enough time at the end of the session to share the feast and say goodbye.

PLANNING THE CHURCH YEAR

We've simplified annual planning by presenting the lessons in their suggested seasonal order of presentation.

In Fall, an opening session on the Church year is followed by Old Testament stories, from creation through the prophets. In Winter, we present the season of Advent and the Feasts of Christmas and Epiphany, followed by the parables. In Spring, we present the Faces of Christ during Lent, followed by Easter presentations of the resurrection, the Eucharist and the early Church.

Not all groups will—or should!—follow this suggested order. Some possible exceptions:
- Groups with regularly scheduled short sessions will need to substitute work sessions for presentations every third or fourth Sunday.
- If the storyteller is not yet comfortable with a particular presentation, we recommend substituting a work session for that day's presentation.
- Within a work session, one child might request the repetition of an earlier presentation. Another child might ask a question that draws on an enrichment presentation; for example, "Why do we have crosses in church?" That's a "teachable moment" to bring out the object box of crosses.

HOW TO MANAGE SPACE

GETTING STARTED

We strongly recommend a thorough reading of *The Complete Guide to Godly Play, Volume 1: How to Lead Godly Play Lessons*.

To start, focus on the relationships and actions that are essential to Godly Play, rather than on the materials needed in a fully equipped Godly Place space. We know that not every parish can allocate generous funds for Christian education. We believe Godly Play is worth beginning with the simplest of resources. Without any materials at all, two teachers can make a Godly Play space that greets the children, shares a feast and blesses them goodbye each week.

When Jerome Berryman began his teaching, he used shelving made from boards and cinder blocks, and only one presentation material: figures for the parable of the Good Shepherd, cut from construction paper and placed in a shoe box he had spray-painted gold.

Over the year, Berryman filled the shelves with additional homemade lesson materials. When more time and money became available, he upgraded those materials to ones cut from foamcore. Now his research room is fully equipped with the full range of beautiful and lasting Godly Play materials: parable boxes, Noah's ark, a desert box filled with sand. All of these riches are wonderful gifts to the children who spend time there, but the *start* of a successful Godly Play environment is the nurturing of appropriate relationships in a safe space.

MATERIALS

MATERIALS FOR PRESENTATIONS

Each lesson details the materials needed in a section titled "Notes on the Materials." You can make materials yourself, or order beautifully crafted materials from:

Godly Play Resources
P.O. Box 563
Ashland, KS 67831
(800) 445-4390
fax: (620) 635-2191
www.godlyplay.com

Here is a list of all suggested materials for the presentations of the Spring quarter:

- *throughout the year (for all or many of the lessons)*
  — circle of the Church year (wall hanging)
  — set of crèche figures
  — cloths in liturgical colors (white, purple, red, green)
  — figure of the Risen Christ
  — juice, fruit and/or cookies
  — matzo

- *Enrichment Lesson: Holy Family*
  — Holy Family figures

— figure of the Risen Christ
— cloths in liturgical colors (white, purple, red, green)

- *Lesson 1: The Mystery of Easter*
  — purple and white bag
  — 6 puzzle pieces

- *Lesson 2: The Faces of Easter I*
  — seven plaques showing Faces of Christ
  — purple and white underlay
  — rack

- *Lesson 3: The Faces of Easter II*
  — seven plaques showing Faces of Christ
  — purple and white underlay
  — rack

- *Lesson 4: The Faces of Easter III*
  — seven plaques showing Faces of Christ
  — purple and white underlay
  — rack

- *Lesson 5: The Faces of Easter IV*
  — seven plaques showing Faces of Christ
  — purple and white underlay
  — rack

- *Lesson 6: The Faces of Easter V*
  — seven plaques showing Faces of Christ
  — purple and white underlay
  — rack

- *Lesson 7: The Faces of Easter VI*
  — seven plaques showing Faces of Christ
  — purple and white underlay
  — rack

- *Lesson 8: The Faces of Easter VII*
  — seven plaques showing Faces of Christ
  — purple and white underlay
  — rack

- *Enrichment Lesson: The Crosses*
  — collection of crosses in a container
  — rug
  — *optional:* cards showing and/or explaining the crosses

- *Enrichment Lesson: Easter Eggs*
  — tray-shaped basket
  — square basket holding 1-3 Ukranian Easter eggs in translucent boxes
  — 1 real (or wooden) egg in a small basket covered with a white cloth
  — collection of 2-dimensional, egg-shaped samples of colors, designs and patterns
  — rug
  — *optional:* plain paper
  — *optional:* plain eggs (wooden or real)
  — *optional:* Easter grass
  — *optional:* small baskets for the children

- *Lesson 9: Jesus and the Twelve*
  — picture of the Last Supper
  — symbols for the 12 apostles
  — control card(s)

- *Lesson 10: The Good Shepherd and World Communion*
  — figures of the Good Shepherd, sheep, sheepfold, table, priest and people of the world
  — small container holding a small paten and chalice
  — 2 circles of green felt

- *Lesson 11: The Synagogue and the Upper Room*
  — model of a synagogue, with a scroll in a basket and a lectern
  — model of the Upper Room with a table
  — figure of Jesus

- *Lesson 12: Circle of the Holy Eucharist*
  — tray-shaped basket
  — card picturing Jesus in the Upper Room
  — card picturing a reader in the synagogue
  — set of 17 cards showing the major parts and acts of the Eucharist
  — green circle

- *Enrichment Lesson: Symbols of the Holy Eucharist*
  — wooden liturgical furnishings (tabernacle, credence table, lectern, altar, pulpit, sacristy cupboard)
  — cloth furnishings (seasonal hangings, fair linen, purificators)
  — other furnishings (Bible, candles, candle sticks, candle snuffer, altar book, gospel book, cruets for water and wine, ciborium, chalice, paten)
  — box of prompting cards

- *Lesson 13: The Mystery of Pentecost*
  — red parable-sized box
  — 12 brown felt strips

— 6 plain wooden blocks
— symbols of the Twelve

• *Lesson 14: Paul's Discovery*
   — box containing 7 cards illustrating scenes from Paul's life
   — 13 scrolls
   — red strip of cloth or felt

• *Lesson 15: The Holy Trinity*
   — materials from the Creation presentation (*The Complete Guide to Godly Play, Volume 2*, Lesson 2, pp. 41-48)
   — materials from the Faces of Easter presentations (this volume, Lessons 2-8, pp. 32-68)
   — materials from Paul's Discovery presentation (this volume, Lesson 14, pp. 126-135)
   — 3 white circles from the Holy Baptism presentation (*The Complete Guide to Godly Play, Volume 3*, Lesson 6, pp. 70-76)

• *Enrichment Lesson: The Part That Hasn't Been Written Yet*
   — book stand
   — blank book

MATERIALS FOR CHILDREN'S WORK

Gather art supplies that the children can use to make their responses. These materials are kept on the art shelves. We suggest:
• paper
• painting trays
• watercolor paints and brushes
• drawing boards
• crayons, pencils and markers
• boards for modeling clay
• clay rolled into small balls in airtight containers

MATERIALS FOR THE FEAST

• napkins
• serving basket
• cups
• tray
• pitcher

MATERIALS FOR CLEANUP

Gather cleaning materials that the children can use to clean up after their work and use to care for their environment. We suggest:

- paper towels
- feather duster
- brush and dustpan
- cleaning cloths
- spray bottles with water
- trash can with liner

HOW TO ARRANGE MATERIALS

The materials are arranged to communicate visually and silently the language system of the Christian faith: our sacred stories, parables and our liturgical actions. Main presentations are generally kept on the top shelves.

Enrichment presentations are generally kept on the second shelves. Bottom shelves are kept free for supplemental materials, such as books, maps or other resources. Separate shelves hold supplies for art, cleanup and the feast. A shelf for children's work in progress is also very important.

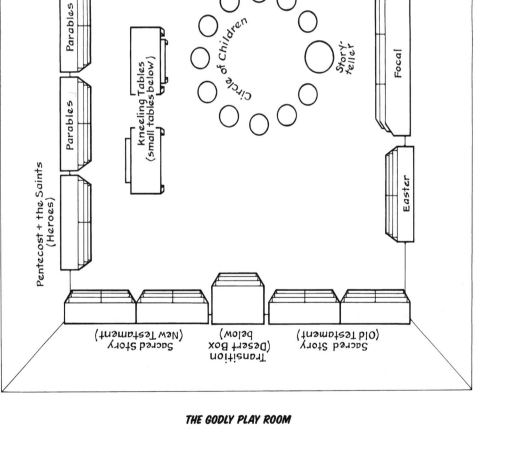

THE GODLY PLAY ROOM

HOW TO MANAGE RELATIONSHIPS

THE TWO TEACHING ROLES:
DOOR PERSON AND STORYTELLER

Each teaching role fosters respect for the children and the Godly Play space. For example, parents are left at the threshold of the Godly Play space and teachers remain at the children's eye level. Both practices keep the room child-centered, instead of adult-centered.

Similarly when the storyteller presents a lesson, he or she keeps eye focus on the materials of the lesson—not the children. Instead of being encouraged to respond to a teacher, the children are invited, by the storyteller's eyes, to enter the story.

In a typical Sunday morning session, only two adults will be present in the Godly Play space: the door person and the storyteller. These are their respective tasks during a typical session:

DOOR PERSON	STORYTELLER
Check the shelves, especially the supply shelves and art shelves.	Check the material to be presented that day.
Get out the roll book, review notes and get ready to greet the children and parents.	Get seated on the floor in the circle and prepare to greet the children.
Slow down the children coming into the room. You may need to take and put aside toys, books and other distracting objects. Help them to get ready. Take the roll or have the older children check themselves in.	Guide the children to places in the circle where they will best be able to attend to the lesson. Visit quietly until it is time to begin and all are ready.
Close the door when it is time. Be ready to work with latecomers and children who come to you from the circle.	Present the lesson. Model how to "enter" the material.
Avoid casual eye contact with the story-teller to help prevent the adults in the room from turning the children into objects, talking down to them or manipulating them.	Draw the children into the lesson by your introduction. Bring your gaze down to focus on the material when you begin the actual lesson. Look up when the wondering begins.

DOOR PERSON

When the children choose their work, they may need help setting up artwork and getting materials from the shelves for work on a lesson, either alone or in a group.

Stay in your chair unless children need your help. Do not intrude on the community of children. Stay at the eye level of the children whenever possible, as if there is a "glass ceiling" in the room at the level of the taller children.

Help the children put their work away, and also help the children who are getting ready to lay out the feast.

Sit quietly in your chair. Be sure that the trash can has a liner in it.

Greet the parents and begin to call the names of the children who are ready and whose parents are there.

If a child starts for the door without saying goodbye to the storyteller, remind him or her to return to the storyteller to say goodbye.

STORYTELLER

After the lesson and wondering, go around the circle, dismissing each child to begin his or her work, one at a time. Each child chooses what to do. Go quickly around the circle the first time, returning to the children who did not decide. Go around the circle for decisions until only a few are left. These may be new or for some other reason cannot make a choice. Present a lesson to these children.

Remain seated in the circle unless children need help with the lessons they have gotten out. You may need to help with art materials. Keep yourself at the children's eye level as you help.

When it is time for the feast, go to the light switch and turn it off. Ask the children to put their work away and come back to the circle for the feast. Turn the light back on. Go to the circle to anchor it as the children finish their work and return.

Ask for prayers, but do not pressure. After the feast, show the children how to put their things away in the trash.

Help the children get ready to have their names called.

As the children's names are called, they come to you. Hold out your hands. Children can take your hands, give a hug or keep their distance, as they like. Tell them quietly and privately how glad you were to see them and what good work they did today. Invite them to come back when they can.

DOOR PERSON

Remember to give back anything that may have been taken at the beginning of class.

When the children are gone, check and clean the art and supply shelves.

Sit quietly and contemplate the session as a whole.

Evaluate, make notes and discuss the session with your coteacher.

STORYTELLER

Take time to enjoy saying goodbye, with all the warmth of a blessing for each child.

When all are gone, check the material shelves and clean.

Sit quietly and contemplate the session as a whole.

Evaluate the session, record your notes and discuss the session with your coteacher.

HOW OTHERS CAN HELP

Other adults who want to support the work of a Godly Play space can contribute by:
- taking turns providing festive and healthy food for the children to share during their feasts
- keeping the art and supply shelves replenished with fresh materials
- using their creative skills to make materials for Godly Play presentations

HOW TO RESPOND EFFECTIVELY TO DISRUPTIONS IN THE CIRCLE

You always want to model the behavior you expect in the circle: focused on the lesson and respectful of everyone in the circle. If a disruption occurs, you deal with that disruption in such a way that you still show continual respect for everyone in the circle—including the child who is having trouble that day. You also still maintain as much focus on the lesson as you can, returning to complete focus on the lesson as quickly as possible.

Therefore, as you consider responses, remember to keep a neutral tone in your voice. Remember, too, that our goal is to help the child move himself or herself toward more appropriate behavior. At the first level of interruption, you might simply raise your eyes from the material. You look up, but not directly at the child, while saying, "We need to get ready again. Watch. This is how we get ready." Model the way to get ready and begin again the presentation where you left off.

If the interruption continues or increases, address the child directly. "No, that's not fair. Look at all these children who are listening. They are ready. You need to be ready, too. Let's try again. Good. That's the way."

If the interruption still continues or increases, ask the child to sit by the door person. Don't think of this as a punishment or as an exclusion from the story: some children *want* to sit by the door person for their own reasons. Continue to keep a neutral tone of voice as you say, "I think you need to sit by Ann. *(Use the door person's name.)* You can see and hear from there. The lesson is still for you."

The goal is for the child to take himself or herself to the door. If the child is having trouble, or says, "No!", you can say, "May I help you?" Only if necessary do you gently pick up the child or, in some similar way, help him or her go to the door person.

HOW TO SUPPORT THE CHILDREN'S WORK

Show respect for the children's work in two key ways: through the structure of the classroom in which the children work and through the language you use—and do *not* use—in talking about their work. Let's explore each of these.

CLASSROOM STRUCTURE

A Godly Play classroom is structured to support children's work in four ways:

- First, it makes *materials* inviting and available by keeping the room open, clean and well-organized. A useful phrase for a Godly Play room is, "This material is for you. You can touch this and work with this when you want to. If you haven't had the lesson, ask one of the other children or the storyteller to show it to you." Children walking into a Godly Play classroom take delight at all the fascinating materials calling out to them. These materials say, "This room is for you."
- Second, it encourages responsible *stewardship* of the shared materials by helping children learn to take care of the room themselves. When something spills, we could quickly wipe it up ourselves, of course. Instead, by helping children learn to take care of their own spills, we communicate to them the respect we have for their own problem-solving capabilities. At the end of work time, each child learns to put away materials carefully. In fact, some children may want to choose cleaning work—dusting or watering plants—for their entire response time.
- Third, it provides a respectful *place* for children's work by reserving space in the room for ongoing or finished projects. When a child is still working on a project at the end of work time, reassure him or her by saying, "This project will be here for you next week. You can take as many weeks as you need to finish it. We never lose work in a Godly Play room." Sometimes children want to give a finished piece of work to the room. Sometimes children want to take either finished or unfinished work home. These choices are theirs to make, and ours to respect.
- Fourth, it sets a leisurely *pace* that allows children to engage deeply in their chosen responses. This is why it's better to do no more than build the circle, share a feast and lovingly say goodbye when we are pressed for time rather than rush through a story and time of art response. When we tell a story, we want to allow enough time

for leisurely wondering together. When we provide work time, we want to allow enough time for children to become deeply engaged in their work. In their wondering or their work, children may be dealing with deep issues—issues that matter as much as life and death. Provide them a nourishing space filled with safe *time* for this deep work.

USING LANGUAGE

You can also support children with the language you use:

- Choose *"open" responses*. We choose "open" responses when we simply describe what we see, rather than evaluate the children or their work. Open responses invite children's interaction, but respect children's choices to simply keep working in silence, too. *Examples:*
  — Hmm. Lots of red.
  — This is big work. The paint goes all the way from here to there.
  — This clay looks so smooth and thin now.
- Avoid *evaluative responses.* Evaluative responses shift the child's focus from his or her work to your praise. In a Godly Play classroom, we want to allow children the freedom to work on what matters most to them, not for the reward of our praise. *Examples to avoid:*
  — You're a wonderful painter.
  — This is a great picture.
  — I'm so pleased with what you did.
- Choose *empowering responses*, which emphasize each child's ability to make choices, solve problems and articulate needs. In a Godly Play classroom, a frequently heard phrase is, "That's the way. You can do this." We encourage children to choose their own work, get the materials out carefully and clean up their work areas when they are done. When a child spills something, respond with, "That's no problem. Do you know where the cleanup supplies are kept?" If a child needs help, show where the supplies are kept or how to wring out a sponge. When helping, the aim is to restore ownership of the problem or situation to the child as soon as possible.
- Stay alert to the children's *needs* during work and cleanup time. The door person's role is especially important as children get out and put away their work. By staying alert to the children's choices in the circle, the door person can know when to help a new child learn the routine for using clay, when a child might need help moving the desert box or when a child might need support in putting material away or cleaning up after painting.

MORE INFORMATION ON GODLY PLAY

The Complete Guide to Godly Play, Volumes 1-4 by Jerome Berryman are available from Living the Good News. *Volume 1: How To Lead Godly Play Lessons* is the essential handbook for using Godly Play in church school or a wide variety of alternative settings. *Volumes 2-4* present complete presentations for Fall, Winter and Spring.

The *Center for the Theology of Childhood* is the nonprofit organization that sponsors ongoing research, training, accreditation programs, the development of a theology of childhood for adults and support of Godly Play. The Center maintains a schedule of training and speaking events related to Godly Play, as well as a list of trainers available throughout this and other countries for help in establishing Godly Play programs.

Contact information:

> Center for the Theology of Childhood at Christ Church Cathedral
> 1117 Texas Avenue
> Houston, TX 77002
> (713) 223-4305
> fax: (713) 223-1041
> e-mail: theologychild2–earthlink.net
> *www.godlyplay.net*

Godly Play Resources crafts beautiful and lasting materials especially for use in a Godly Play classroom. Although you can make your own materials, many teachers find their work both simplified and enriched by using Godly Play Resources to supply their classrooms. *Contact information:*

> Godly Play Resources
> P.O. Box 563
> Ashland, KS 67831
> (800) 445-4390
> fax: (620) 635-2191
> *www.godlyplay.com*

ENRICHMENT LESSON
THE HOLY FAMILY

LESSON NOTES
FOCUS: AXIS OF THE CHRISTIAN LANGUAGE SYSTEM: THE BIRTH, LIFE, DEATH AND RESURRECTION OF JESUS CHRIST

● LITURGICAL ACTION

● ENRICHMENT PRESENTATION

THE MATERIAL

● LOCATION: FOCAL SHELVES

● PIECES: HOLY FAMILY FIGURES AND FIGURE OF THE RISEN CHRIST

● UNDERLAY: NONE

BACKGROUND

We first present this lesson at the beginning of the church-school year. We repeat the lesson whenever we change the liturgical colors in the room to reflect the changes in the liturgical season—purple or blue for Advent, white for Christmas, green for Epiphany and so on. On those occasions, one purpose of the lesson is simple: we take the Holy Family off the shelf, change the colored cloth on the shelf to a new one, then replace the figures on the new cloth.

However, the Holy Family holds deep significance for our work throughout the year. That is why it sits right in the center of the focal shelves in the room—right behind the storyteller—every week of the year. That is why we draw attention to it in this presentation to the children every time we change liturgical colors. The Holy Family is the *matrix*—the Latin word for womb—out of which new life comes. This story is the story of the re-creation of the universe. Christ's incarnation changes everything. Most especially, it changes the way we understand ourselves, each other, the Creator and the created world around us.

We find existential meaning in our lives, in the places into which we are born, through the network of these relationships. The "answer" to life is not a propositional statement or verbal key. Instead of an answer, we find a "home," every day, in the midst of these relationships of love and creating.

The axis of life in the Christian tradition is birth-death-rebirth. The children begin to perceive this axis through the naming of the Holy Family, and through the careful, respectful moving of the figures. We do not talk about this meaning, but wait for the children themselves to discover it. We, like the Holy Family, are invited to be cocreators in the biological, psychological, social and spiritual spheres of life.

NOTES ON THE MATERIAL

The material is a Nativity set with these figures: Mary, Joseph, the Christ Child (removable, with outstretched arms), a shepherd, one or more sheep, a donkey, a cow and the three kings, together with a figure of the Risen Christ with outstretched arms. Any size will do, but 4"-6" figures work well for young children. Children can easily handle these small figures, and they won't take up as much room on the shelf. Behind the Holy Family, place the Risen Christ with outstretched arms.

If possible, find figures that are not too detailed or realistic, so that children can supply details through their imaginations. More figures or more complex figures will not work as well as the simple set described above. Don't include a stable; it distracts from the Holy Family.

In an ideal setup, the focal shelves are the shelving unit directly opposite the door through which the children enter. The Holy Family sits in the center of the top shelf. To the right of the Holy Family, also on the top shelf, is the green circle with the figure of the Good Shepherd and his sheep, from the material for World Communion (see pp. 91-98). To the left of the Holy Family stands a tall white candle called the Light (or the Christ Candle).

On the shelves below the Good Shepherd are the remaining materials for the World Communion lesson. Below the Light on the second shelf are the remaining materials for the lesson about Holy Baptism (see *The Complete Guide to Godly Play, Volume 3*). Below the Holy Family on the second shelf is a tray that contains the colored cloths of the liturgical year and a circular tray lined with white felt. You will use these two trays whenever you change liturgical colors during the year. On the bottom shelf is the material for the Circle of the Church Year (see *The Complete Guide to Godly Play, Volume 2,* Lesson 1, pp. 23-33).

SPECIAL NOTES

Classroom Management: Children can use the felt-lined tray when they work with the Holy Family, but most children will prefer to keep the figures on the top focal shelf as they move them around.

We suggest you tell this story at least twice in the Spring season. On the first Sunday of Lent, use the story to change the cloth underneath the Holy Family from green to purple. On the first Sunday you meet during the season of Easter, use the story to change the cloth underneath the Holy Family from purple to white. If you meet on the Day of Pentecost, you can change the cloth to red. If you have any meetings after the Easter season, use the story to change the cloth to green.

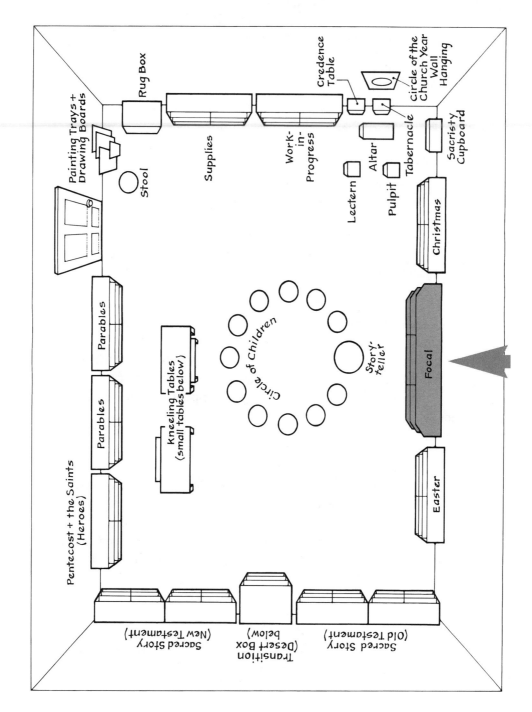

WHERE TO FIND MATERIALS

MOVEMENTS

The storyteller sits in front of the focal shelves. In the center of the top shelf is the Holy Family, which rests on a cloth colored to match the liturgical time of year—red for Pentecost, white for Easter, and so on. Behind the Holy Family, there is a picture or carving of the Risen Christ.

Tell this story whenever you want to change the color of the cloth underneath the Holy Family, the focal point of the room throughout the year. For this lesson, the Holy Family is already resting on a green cloth. In this telling, you will change the cloth to purple or blue, to match the liturgical color used in your church for Advent.

When the children are settled in the circle, you begin. Go to the rug box and get a rug. Return to the circle and roll it out. Turn and take out the round tray for the Holy Family from the lower shelves behind you. It is large enough to hold all the figures of the Holy Family. The bottom of the tray is covered with white felt.

Move to the side so the children can see the Holy Family on the shelf behind you. Turn toward the shelf and open your hands to show what you are going to talk about. Wait until you are present to the story yourself before beginning.

Pick up the Christ Child from the manger and hold it in the palm of your hand for all the children to see.

WORDS

This is the Holy Family. Sometimes when you see something like this, it is not for children to touch. It might break easily, so you need to ask if you can touch it or work with it. This Holy Family is for you. It is for you to touch and work with. You don't need to ask to work with it.

This is the Christ Child. He is holding out his arms to give you a hug.

MOVEMENTS **WORDS**

THE HOLY FAMILY

MOVEMENTS	WORDS
Put the manger on the white circle tray in front of you. Replace the Christ Child in the manger.	
Hold Mary in the palm of your hand as well, showing her to the children. Then place her behind the manger, looking across it to the children.	Here is the Mother Mary.
Hold Joseph in the palm of your hand and then place him next to Mary.	Here is the Father Joseph.
Hold out the donkey and then place it beside Mary.	Here is the donkey that Mary rode when she and Joseph went to Bethlehem to be counted by the Roman soldiers. Mary was about to have a baby, so it was hard for her to walk. Sometimes she rode on the donkey. It is also hard to ride on a donkey when you are about to have a baby, so she got down again and walked.
Hold out the cow and then place it beside Joseph.	Here is the cow that was in the stable when the baby was born. He was surprised to find a baby in the feed box, the manger, where he usually found his breakfast.
Hold out the shepherd and sheep and then place them facing toward the Christ Child on the other side of the manger from Mary and Joseph.	Here is the shepherd who saw the great light in the sky at night. There were more shepherds than this, but we will put down one to remind us. Here are some of the sheep. There were more, but these will do to help us remember.

MOVEMENTS	WORDS
	When they saw the light in the darkness, they were afraid. I would be, too. Then they heard singing. That scared them, too, until they heard the words. The angels sang that they came to bring peace on earth and good will to all people. "Run. Hurry. Go to Bethlehem. Something has happened there that changes everything!"
Hold out the three Magi and place them as you speak.	Here are the three kings, the wise men. They were so wise that people thought they were magic. In their language they were called the Magi, and that word is the word from which we get our word *magic.* They knew so much that people thought they were magic. And of all the things they knew, they knew the most about the stars.
	One day they saw the wild star. The Magi knew where all the stars were supposed to be in the sky, but this star moved. This star was not on their maps of the sky. So when it moved, they were curious, and followed it. It led them to the stable where the Christ Child was born.
	The wise men brought with them gifts for the Christ Child: gold, frankincense and myrrh.
Pick up the Christ Child from the manger. Hold out the Christ Child to the children and continue holding him as you speak.	Here is the little baby reaching out to give you a hug. He grew up to be a man and died on the cross. That is very sad, but it is also wonderful, in an Easter kind of way.
Move the Christ Child slowly and with dignity to the figure of the Risen Christ. Superimpose the baby with outstretched arms on the Risen Christ's outstretched arms.	Now he can reach out and give the whole world a hug. He is not just back then, in this place or that place. He is everywhere, and in every time.

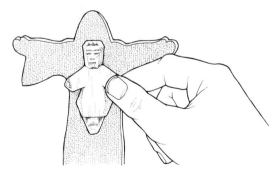

THE CHRIST CHILD AND THE RISEN CHRIST

MOVEMENTS

Return the Christ Child to the manger. Sit back and quietly take in the whole scene. Be present to its meaning.

Roll up the green underlay from the top shelf of the focal shelves. Place it on the tray of liturgical cloths on the middle shelf of the focal shelves. From this same tray, take out the purple cloth and roll it out on the top shelf.

You now begin to replace the Holy Family, one by one, without hurrying, naming each one as you slowly and with care put them back on the purple cloth. (Whether placing the figures on the white tray, or returning them to the focal shelf, use the layout illustrated on p. 24.)

Pause and then begin the wondering with the children.

Sit back as the wondering draws to a close. Enjoy what has been said and done. Then begin to go around the circle to help the children choose their work, one at a time.

WORDS

⟹ Here is the Baby Jesus.
Here is the Mother Mary.
Here is the Father Joseph.
Here is the donkey that Mary rode on.
Here is the cow that was so surprised in the morning.
Here is one of the shepherds and a few of the sheep.
Here are the wise men, the three kings, the Magi.

This is the Holy Family, and you can work with these figures any time you wish. In our classroom, they are for you.

⟹ Now I wonder what part of the Holy Family you like best?

I wonder what part of the Holy Family is the most important part?

I wonder if you have ever seen any of the Holy Family in our church?

I wonder if there is any of the Holy Family we can leave out and still have all we need?

⟹ Now it is time to get out our work. What work would you like to get out today? You may work with the Holy Family, or you may make something about them. Maybe you have something that you are already working on. There may be another material you would like to work with. There is so much. While I am going around the circle, think about what you are going to work with.

LESSON 1
THE MYSTERY OF EASTER

FOCUS: LENT, THE MYSTERY OF EASTER AND THE EASTER SEASON

- LITURGICAL ACTION
- CORE PRESENTATION

THE MATERIAL

- LOCATION: EASTER SHELVES
- PIECES: PURPLE AND WHITE BAG, SIX PUZZLE PIECES
- UNDERLAY: NONE

BACKGROUND

Lent is the season when we prepare for Easter. These six weeks are a solemn time, overflowing with meaning, when we view life from the perspective of our existential limits and the sacrifice of Christ. This lesson gives an introduction to the relationship of Lent to the Mystery of Easter as well as how Easter overflows into the *season* of Easter. Follow this introduction by presenting the lessons of the Faces of Easter during the weeks of Lent.

NOTES ON THE MATERIAL

Find the materials for this presentation on the top shelf of the Easter shelves. To the right will be the material for the Faces of Easter.

A bag, which is purple on the outside and white on the inside, holds six puzzle pieces, which, when assembled, make the shape of the cross. One side of the cross is purple; the other side of the cross is white. It is much more than a puzzle with pieces that fit together, as you will see from how the lesson ends in the Mystery and season of Easter.

SPECIAL NOTES

Storytelling Tip: Remember that this story is called the Mystery of *Easter*, not the Mystery of Lent. The fullest meaning of Lent is that it gives us time to prepare for the great Mystery of Easter, the principal feast of the Christian Church. Similarly, we recommend that you not call the material a "cross puzzle" but always refer to it as "the material for the Mystery of Easter."

On the First Sunday of Lent, we recommend that you first focus on the change of seasons. Use the Holy Family presentation to change the focal shelf color from green to purple. Then tell the Mystery of Easter. Most often, that will be all the material suitable for the First Sunday of Lent. You can combine two of the Faces presentations on the next Sunday.

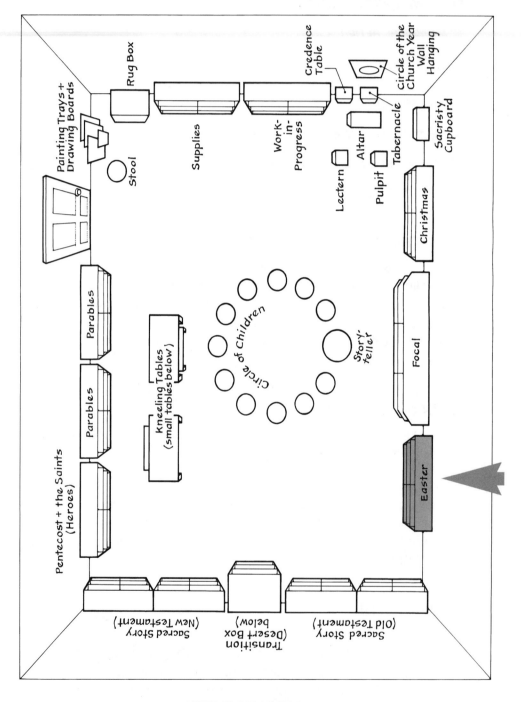

WHERE TO FIND MATERIALS

MOVEMENTS	WORDS
Go to the Easter shelves and bring the tray with the bag on it. Put the tray at your side and place the bag in the middle of the circle. Unless you have a rug larger than the assembled cross, tell this lesson without a rug.	Watch carefully where I go so you will always know where to find this lesson.
Pick up the bag and explore it from the outside.	Now is the time for the color purple. It is the time for preparing. Purple is the color of kings. We are preparing for the coming of a king and his going and his coming again. We are preparing for the Mystery of Easter.
	This is a serious time. It takes many weeks to get ready to enter the Mystery of Easter. Let's look inside to see how many weeks it takes and what Lent makes when it is all put together.
Place the bag back on the floor and reach inside. Pull out the first piece with the purple side up. Place it beside the bag. Turn it this way and that.	I wonder what this could be?
Encourage the children's guesses, then reach inside the bag and take out a second piece.	Look. Here is a second piece. I wonder what this could be?
Place the second piece on the floor, apart from the first piece. Turn the pieces, but do not fit them together.	
Take out the third piece. Put the third piece beside the other two, but do not fit the pieces together. Move the pieces around and try combinations that do not work.	Look. Here's a third piece. They are all so different.
Take out the fourth piece. Put the fourth piece beside the other three, but do not fit the pieces together.	Here is a fourth piece. One, two, three, four weeks in Lent? That's the same as the time for getting ready for Christmas. Perhaps that is all we need for Easter, too.
Take out the fifth piece.	Oh, no! Here's another one. Lent is longer than Advent. The Mystery of Easter is an even greater mystery than the Mystery of Christmas, so it must take longer to get ready.

MOVEMENTS	WORDS
Touch the almost empty bag and "find" yet another piece.	That must be all there is. No. It is not empty. There must be another week inside.
Take out the sixth piece.	There *is* another one! The time of Lent is six weeks. Easter is a huge mystery. Let's see if there is another one.

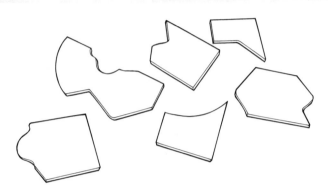

THE PIECES OF THE CROSS PUZZLE

Look in the bag. It is now empty. Place the bag on the floor and sit back to wonder about it.	Lent helps us to get ready. It is a time to know more about the One who is Easter. It is also a time to learn more about who we really are.
Touch one or more of the pieces as you talk about them.	The pieces are very purple. The One who is coming is very important, like a king. But purple can feel kind of sad, too. Perhaps what is going to happen is sad.
Begin to move the pieces around, but do not yet fit them together. Experiment. Propose alternative constructions. Play.	I wonder what all these make when you put them all together?
Finally, assemble the cross.	Oh, I see. It makes the cross, a serious cross. It is also sad. Jesus grew up to be a man and died on the cross. That *is* sad, but it is also wonderful.

Now look what happens. |
Turn the pieces over to make a completely white cross.	Jesus died on the cross, but somehow he is still with us. That is why Easter is not just sad. It is also wonderful.
Show the purple side of a few pieces.	Lent is sad...
Turn the pieces back to white again.	...Easter is pure celebration.

MOVEMENTS

WORDS

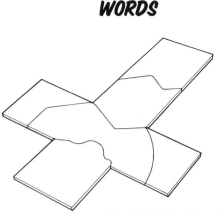

THE ASSEMBLED CROSS (STORYTELLER'S PERSPECTIVE)

Reach inside the purple bag and take hold of the inside. Turn the bag inside out.

Easter turns everything inside out and upside down. The color of getting ready becomes the color of pure celebration. The sad seriousness and happiness join together to make joy.

Count the white pieces.

Look! You can't keep Easter in just one Sunday! It goes on for one, two, three, four, five, six weeks! All the way to Pentecost.

Sit back and contemplate the Mystery of Easter for a few moments, and then begin the wondering questions.

Now I wonder if you have ever seen these colors in the church?

I wonder what happens when you see these colors?

I wonder what part of Lent you like best?

I wonder what part of Lent is the most important?

I wonder who takes care of the colors?

I wonder where these colors are when you don't see them?

I wonder if you see the white at some other time in church?

I wonder how sadness and happiness can make joy?

I wonder where joy comes from?

I wonder how you know when joy is here?

When the wondering is finished, put the pieces of the cross inside the bag, leaving it with the white on the outside. Return the material to the shelf and help the children begin to get out their work.

The Mystery of Easter 31

LESSON 2
THE FACES OF EASTER I

LESSON NOTES
FOCUS: JESUS' BIRTH AND GROWTH

- LITURGICAL ACTION
- CORE PRESENTATION

THE MATERIAL

- LOCATION: EASTER SHELVES
- PIECES: SEVEN PLAQUES ILLUSTRATED WITH FACES OF CHRIST, WITH RACK
- UNDERLAY: PURPLE AND WHITE

BACKGROUND

Lent is the season when we prepare for Easter. This lesson helps children prepare for the Mystery of Easter. We move toward the Mystery by hearing the stories of Christ's journey toward the cross and resurrection. This week's presentation focuses on the face of Christ as a newborn child. If you used the presentations of the Holy Family and the Mystery of Easter on the first week of Lent, then you might want to tell two of the Faces presentations today.

NOTES ON THE MATERIAL

Find the materials for this presentation in the middle of the top shelf of the Easter shelves, in between the material for the Mystery of Easter, and the Synagogue and the Upper Room.

The material consists of a set of seven faces of Christ, mounted on wood or card-stock plaques. The underlay is a purple and white "scroll" that unrolls to show six purple rectangles and one white rectangle. Roll up the underlay so that the white rectangle is hidden inside.

A special carrier rack for the Faces plaques stands them up, making them visible to a child scanning the room full of materials. This stand for the plaques also holds the rolled-up underlay. If you do not use this stand, put the rolled-up underlay and plaques in a tray.

THE EASTER PLAQUES

SPECIAL NOTES

Storytelling Tip: At the end of each presentation of the Faces stories, you invite children to choose materials from the room that will help tell more of the story. For example, when you tell today's story of "Jesus' Birth and Growth," one child might bring crèche figures to place by the plaque. Another child might bring the desert box. Be open to the surprising connections children make as they explore the meaning embodied in the materials. This activity is especially important because it provides movement and action to these stories and integrates the whole room with Jesus' birth, life, death and resurrection.

Be sure you unroll the underlay so that its roll is closest to you, not to the children. This keeps the roll from blocking some of the children's view of the Faces. (See the illustration, p. 36.) The underlay unrolls toward the storyteller, so you also need to pull the unrolled portion toward the children. It is as if the story is growing out of the rolled up underlay like a seed, the white part rolled up inside. It also is growing out of the storyteller's life and experience toward the children The illustrations in these sessions make this clear. Each time you present any of the Faces of Easter, unroll the underlay, place the first plaque, unroll the underlay, place the second plaque, etc.

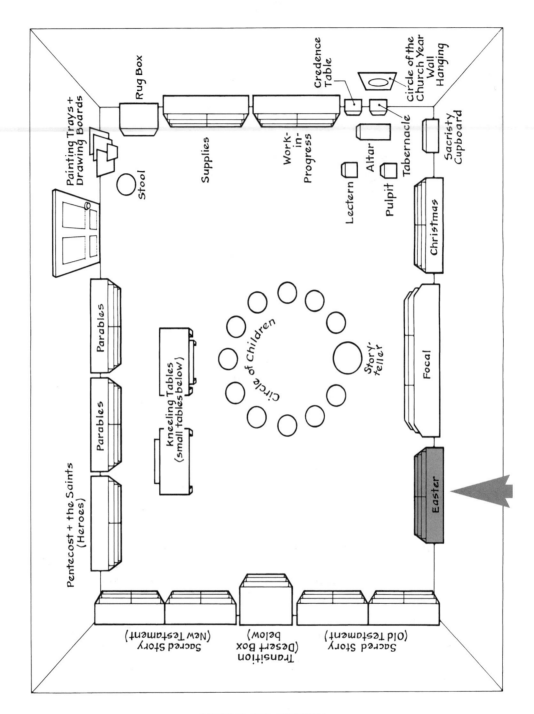

WHERE TO FIND MATERIALS

MOVEMENTS

When the children are ready, go to the shelf where the Lent and Easter materials are kept. Bring the plaques and rolled-up underlay "scroll" to the circle.

Put the cards at your side and place the scroll in front of you. Unroll the underlay toward the children to uncover the rectangle for the first plaque.

Pick up the first plaque, with the picture of the infant Jesus, and hold the face toward the children. Point to the figures as you identify them and trace around their faces.

WORDS

▶ Watch carefully where I go so you will always know where to find this lesson.

▶ In the beginning, the baby was born. God chose Mary to be the Mother of God. Listen carefully! Listen to the words.

God chose Mary to be the Mother of God, and the Word was born a wordless child.

HOLDING THE FIRST PLAQUE (CHILDREN'S PERSPECTIVE)

In Mary's face, trace the cross with your index finger along the line of the nose to the mouth, and then the line from eye to eye. Repeat for Joseph's face.

▶ When the baby looked up into the face of the Mother Mary, he already saw the cross. When he looked into the face of the Father Joseph, the cross was there, too.

Trace a circle around the whole family.

▶ The Mother Mary and the Father Joseph held the baby close. They kept the baby warm. They gave the baby everything the baby needed to grow, and it began to grow.

When you have enjoyed for a moment the idea of the baby growing, put the plaque down on the underlay, facing the children.

▶ Now I wonder if there is anything in this room that you can bring and put beside this picture to help us tell more about this part of the story. Look around and see. I will go around the circle and ask each one of you if you would like to go and get something to put beside the picture of the Christ Child to show more of the story.

MOVEMENTS

WORDS

THE FIRST PLAQUE ON THE UNDERLAY (STORYTELLER'S PERSPECTIVE)

Begin to go around the circle, asking each child if he or she would like to bring something to put by the plaque. Some children may not be able to think of anything, so move on if it looks as if they are stuck. You can come back to them later. If they are still stuck, that is okay. Many children learn by watching as well as by doing.

I don't know what you are going to get. You are the only one in the world who knows that.

If you don't feel like getting something, that's okay. Just enjoy what we make together.

Sometimes children get up, wander for a moment and bring something at random, without knowing why. That's okay. Be amazed (which is easy) and wonder why with them, together coming up with something relevant. Everything in the room is connected in some way.

Enjoy the items that the children bring to help tell the story. When you have had time to enjoy the entire layout, invite children, one at a time, to return their materials to their places on the shelves. Then take the plaques and underlay back to the Easter shelves.

Help the children begin to get out their work.

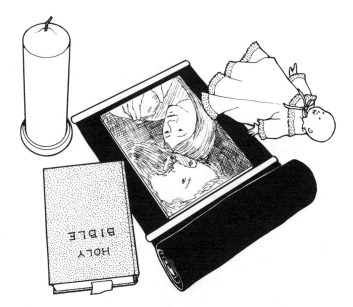

THE FIRST PLAQUE WITH ITEMS CHOSEN BY THE CHILDREN (STORYTELLER'S PERSPECTIVE)

LESSON 3

THE FACES OF EASTER II

LESSON NOTES

FOCUS: JESUS IS LOST AND FOUND

- LITURGICAL ACTION
- CORE PRESENTATION

THE MATERIAL

- LOCATION: EASTER SHELVES
- PIECES: SEVEN PLAQUES ILLUSTRATED WITH FACES OF CHRIST, WITH RACK
- UNDERLAY: PURPLE AND WHITE

BACKGROUND

Lent is the season when we prepare for Easter. This lesson continues to help children prepare for the Mystery of Easter. We move toward the Mystery by hearing the stories of Christ's journey toward the cross and resurrection. This week's presentation focuses on the face of Christ as the One who was lost and found.

Begin this week's presentation by presenting a summary of the first plaque, the Face of "Jesus' Birth and Growth" (pp. 32-36). Then add the second plaque and tell the story found in this second lesson about the Faces of Easter.

Since there are seven Faces presentations and only six Sundays in Lent, you may want to combine presentations, telling two or even three stories on a Sunday. Arrange the presentations to fit your church's religious education schedule or other situations.

NOTES ON THE MATERIAL

Find the materials for this presentation in the middle of the top shelf of the Easter shelves, in between the material for the Mystery of Easter, and the Synagogue and the Upper Room.

The material consists of a set of seven faces of Christ, mounted on wood or card-stock plaques. The underlay is a purple and white "scroll" that unrolls to show six purple rectangles and one white rectangle. Roll up the underlay so that the white rectangle is hidden inside.

A special carrier rack for the Faces plaques stands them up, making them visible to a child scanning the room full of materials. This stand for the plaques should also hold the rolled-up underlay. (See the illustration on p. 33.) If you do not use this stand, put the rolled-up underlay and plaques in a tray.

SPECIAL NOTES

Storytelling Tip: At the end of each presentation of the Faces stories, you invite children to choose materials from the room that will help tell more of the story. This activity helps children perceive connections between the stories. Because you add a story each week, only invite children to bring materials for that week's story. For example, when you tell today's story of the Face of "Jesus Is Lost and Found," one child might bring Solomon's Temple to place by the plaque.

Be sure you unroll the underlay so that its roll is toward you, not toward the children. This keeps the roll from blocking some of the children's view of the Faces. The underlay unrolls toward the storyteller; each new plaque will be placed on the underlay closest to the storyteller. This means that you need to slide the underlay away from you to allow room to unroll the next section of the underlay. (See the illustration, p. 41.) A child seated across from you can help pull the underlay away from you.

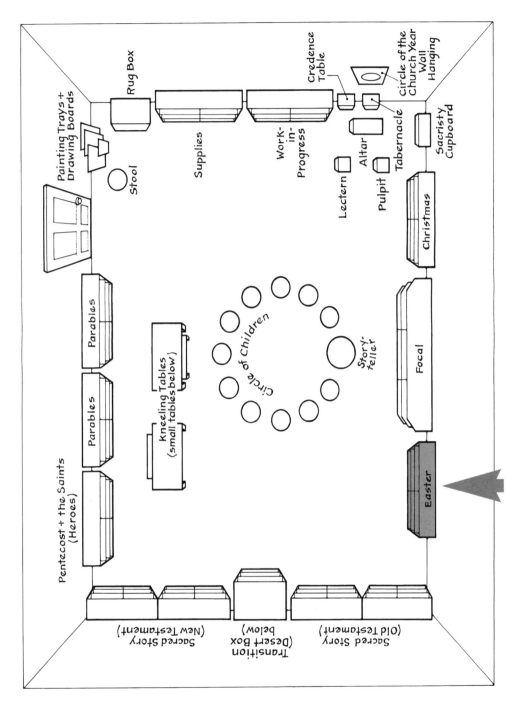

WHERE TO FIND MATERIALS

i wonder

MOVEMENTS

When the children are ready, go to the Easter shelves and bring the plaques and rolled-up underlay to the circle.

Put the cards at your side and place the underlay in front of you. Unroll the underlay toward you to uncover the rectangle for the first plaque. Tell in summary the story "Jesus' Birth and Growth" (pp. 35-36). When you are finished, lay down the first plaque.

Unroll the underlay to uncover the second section. Pick up the second plaque and hold it so that the children can see it as you continue the story:

WORDS

Watch carefully where I go so you will always know where to find this lesson.

The baby grew and became a boy. When he was about twelve years old, he went with the Mother Mary and the Father Joseph and with many other people from their village of Nazareth to the great city of Jerusalem to keep one of the high, holy days. When the celebration was over, the people from Nazareth went out through the great high gate and started on the road toward home.

Suddenly, Mary and Joseph discovered that Jesus was not there! They thought he had been playing with the other children from their village as they walked together. They hurried back into the great city of Jerusalem to find him.

Mary and Joseph looked in the dark and narrow streets. They looked in the marketplace where they had bought their food. They looked where they had spent the night. They looked everywhere!

Finally, they even looked in the Temple—and there he was. He was talking to the rabbis, the priests. When he spoke, they listened, because he knew so much. When they spoke, he listened, because he wanted to learn more.

Mary and Joseph then asked Jesus the question all parents ask their children, the question you can never answer: "Why did you do this?" And Jesus said something very strange. He said, "Didn't you know I would be in my Father's house?"

Mary and Joseph did not understand. Their house was in Nazareth, where Joseph's carpenter shop was. They did not understand, but they did not forget.

MOVEMENTS

Put the second plaque down on the second rectangle of the underlay, facing the children.

WORDS

Now I wonder what there is in our room that can help us tell more about this part of the story. Look around and see if you see something. I will go around the circle and invite you to go and get something to put by the picture of the boy who was lost and found to help us tell more.

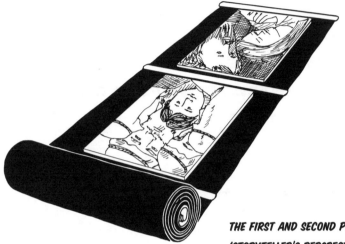

THE FIRST AND SECOND PLAQUES ON THE UNDERLAY (STORYTELLER'S PERSPECTIVE)

Begin to go around the circle, inviting each child to bring something to put by the plaque illustrating "Jesus Is Lost and Found." Some children may not be able to think of anything, so move on if it looks as if they are stuck. You can come back to them later. If they are still stuck, that is okay. Many children learn by watching as well as by doing.

Enjoy the items that the children bring to help tell more of the story. When you have had time to enjoy the entire layout, invite children, one at a time, to return their materials. Then take the plaques and underlay back to the Easter shelves.

Help the children begin to get out their work.

LESSON 4

THE FACES OF EASTER III

FOCUS: JESUS' BAPTISM AND BLESSING BY GOD

- **LITURGICAL ACTION**
- **CORE PRESENTATION**

THE MATERIAL

- **LOCATION: EASTER SHELVES**
- **PIECES: SEVEN PLAQUES ILLUSTRATED WITH FACES OF CHRIST, WITH RACK**
- **UNDERLAY: PURPLE AND WHITE**

BACKGROUND

Lent is the season when we prepare for Easter. This lesson continues to help children prepare for the Mystery of Easter. We move toward the Mystery by hearing the stories of Christ's journey toward the cross and resurrection. This week's presentation focuses on the face of Christ as the One who was baptized and blessed.

You begin this week's presentation by presenting a summary of the first two plaques, the Face of "Jesus' Birth and Growth" (pp. 32-36) and the Face of "Jesus Is Lost and Found" (pp. 37-41). Begin with those two presentations before adding the third plaque and its story.

NOTES ON THE MATERIAL

Find the materials for this presentation in the middle of the top shelf of the Easter shelves, in between the material for the Mystery of Easter, and the Synagogue and the Upper Room.

The material consists of a set of seven faces of Christ, mounted on wood or card-stock plaques. The underlay is a purple and white "scroll" that unrolls to show six purple rectangles and one white rectangle. Roll up the underlay so that the white rectangle is hidden inside.

A special carrier rack for the Faces plaques stands them up, making them visible to a child scanning the room full of materials. This stand for the plaques also holds the rolled-up underlay. (See the illustration on p. 33.) If you do not use this stand, put the rolled-up underlay and plaques in a tray.

SPECIAL NOTES

At Home: The Faces of Easter also work well as a presentation for family storytelling around the table during Lent. Instead of inviting listeners to bring other materials to the story, finish by asking special wondering questions. For example, for these first three presentations, you could ask:

- I wonder if there was anyone here who was ever born?
- I wonder if anyone around this table was every lost? Found?
- I wonder if there is anyone in this family who was baptized?

This kind of storytelling gathers the family and its stories within the context of the Master Story of the Christian People.

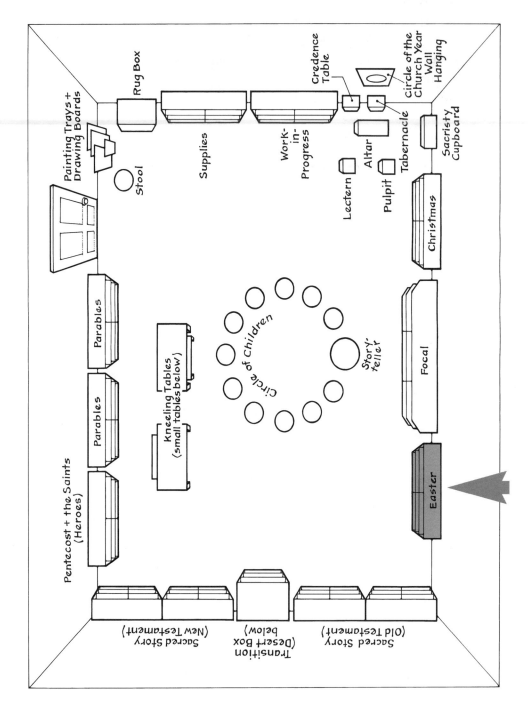

WHERE TO FIND MATERIALS

MOVEMENTS

When the children are ready, go to the Easter shelves and bring the plaques and rolled-up underlay to the circle.

Put the cards at your side and place the underlay in front of you. Unroll the underlay toward you to uncover the rectangle for the first plaque. Tell in summary the story "Jesus' Birth and Growth" (pp. 32-36). When you are finished, lay down the first plaque.

Unroll the underlay to uncover the rectangle for the second plaque. Tell in summary the story "Jesus Is Lost and Found" (pp. 37-41). When you are finished, lay down the second plaque.

Unroll the underlay to uncover the third rectangle. Pick up the third plaque and hold it so that the children can see it as you tell this story:

Point to John. All you can see is his hair.

Cover Jesus' face with one of your hands. Remove your hand. Trace the outline of the dove at the top of the plaque.

WORDS

Watch carefully where I go so you will always know where to find this lesson.

Jesus grew and became a man. When he was about thirty years old, he went to the River Jordan, where his cousin, John, was baptizing people.

Do you see John? You can just see the back of his head. He was a wild man!

Jesus waded into the river until he was face to face with John. He said, "Baptize me."

John looked at Jesus as if for the first time. Now he saw who he really was. "How can I baptize you? You are the Messiah, the one we have been waiting for. You must baptize me."

"No. It is written that you will come before me and prepare the way. Baptize me."

Jesus went down into the darkness and chaos of the water. When John lifted him back up into the light, there were people there who said they saw a dove come down from heaven and come close to him.

MOVEMENTS

WORDS

There were also people there that day who heard a voice. The voice said, "This is my beloved son, with whom I am well pleased."

After Jesus was baptized, he went on across the River Jordan into the desert. He stayed there for forty days and forty nights to learn more about who he was and what his work was going to be.

Put the third plaque down on the third rectangle of the underlay, with the face of Jesus toward the children.

Now I wonder what there is in this room that can help us tell more of the story. Look around and see if you see something. I will go around the circle and invite each one of you to go and get something to put by the picture to help us show more of the story.

THE FIRST, SECOND AND THIRD PLAQUES ON THE UNDERLAY (STORYTELLER'S PERSPECTIVE)

Begin to go around the circle, asking each child if he or she would like to bring something to put by the plaque illustrating "Jesus' Baptism and Blessing by God." Some children may not be able to think of anything, so move on, coming back to them later. If they are still stuck, that is okay. Many children learn by watching as well as by doing.

Enjoy the items that the children bring. When you have had time to enjoy the entire layout, invite children, one at a time, to return their materials. Then take the plaques and underlay back to the Easter shelves.

Help the children choose their work.

LESSON 5

THE FACES OF EASTER IV

LESSON NOTES

FOCUS: JESUS' DESERT AND DISCOVERY EXPERIENCE

- ● LITURGICAL ACTION
- ● CORE PRESENTATION

THE MATERIAL

- ● LOCATION: EASTER SHELVES
- ● PIECES: SEVEN PLAQUES ILLUSTRATED WITH FACES OF CHRIST, WITH RACK
- ● UNDERLAY: PURPLE AND WHITE

BACKGROUND

Lent is the season when we prepare for Easter. This lesson continues to help children prepare for the Mystery of Easter. We move toward the Mystery by hearing the stories of Christ's journey toward the cross and resurrection. This week's presentation focuses on Christ's temptations in the desert.

You will begin this week's presentation by presenting a summary of the first three plaques:
- Jesus' Birth and Growth (pp. 32-36)
- Jesus Is Lost and Found (pp. 37-41)
- Jesus' Baptism and Blessing by God (pp. 42-46)

Begin with those three presentations before adding the fourth plaque and its story.

NOTES ON THE MATERIAL

Find the materials for this presentation in the middle of the top shelf of the Easter shelves, in between the material for the Mystery of Easter and the Synagogue and the Upper Room.

The material consists of a set of seven faces of Christ, mounted on wood or card-stock plaques. The underlay is a purple and white "scroll" that unrolls to show six purple rectangles and one white rectangle. Roll up the underlay so that the white rectangle is hidden inside.

A special carrier rack for the Faces plaques stands them up, making them visible to a child scanning the room full of materials. This stand for the plaques should also holds the rolled-up underlay. (See the illustration on p. 33.) If you do not use this stand, put the rolled-up underlay and plaques in a tray.

SPECIAL NOTES

Storytelling Tips: Inviting children to bring materials to put next to the stories introduces a technique of "side by side" connections. You can tell two Godly Play stories together and invite children to make their own links. This works especially well with older children. For example, you could tell the creation story (see *The Complete Guide To Godly Play, Volume Two,* pp. 41-48) side by side with the Faces stories. Ask children, for example, "I wonder where this day (from the Creation) belongs in this story (the Faces)?"

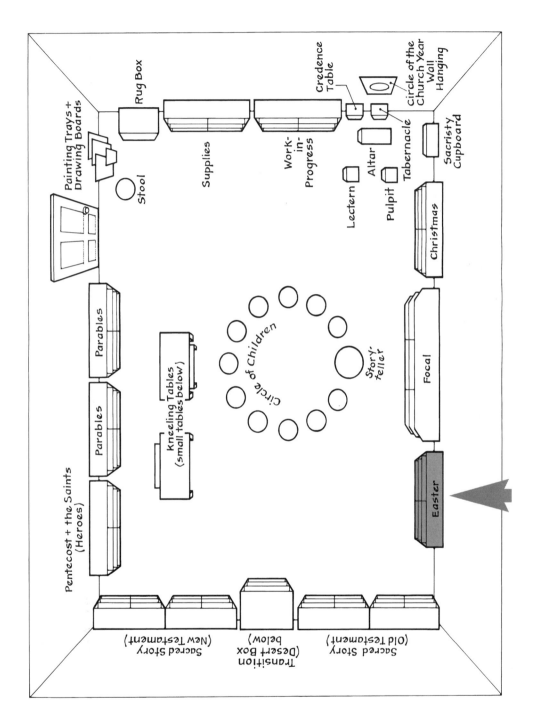

WHERE TO FIND MATERIALS

MOVEMENTS

When the children are ready, go to the Easter shelves and bring the plaques and rolled-up underlay to the circle.

Put the cards at your side and place the underlay in front of you. Unroll the underlay toward you to uncover the rectangle for the first plaque. Tell in summary the story "Jesus' Birth and Growth" (pp. 32-36). When you are finished, lay down the first plaque.

Unroll the underlay to uncover the rectangle for the second plaque. Tell in summary the story "Jesus Is Lost and Found" (pp. 37-41). When you are finished, lay down the second plaque.

Unroll the underlay to uncover the rectangle for the third plaque. Tell in summary the story "Jesus' Baptism and Blessing by God" (pp. 42-46). When you are finished, lay down the third plaque.

Unroll the underlay to uncover the fourth section. Pick up the fourth plaque and hold it so that the children can see it as you tell this story:

WORDS

▸ Watch carefully where I go so you will always know where to find this lesson.

▸ Jesus went into the desert to discover more about who he was and what his work was going to be. He was there for forty days and forty nights. There was little to eat or to drink.

One day he heard a voice. It said, "Why don't you turn one of those stones over there into bread and have something to eat?"

Jesus said, "No. To be a real human being, we need more than just bread to eat."

Suddenly, it was as if Jesus were on top of the great Temple in Jerusalem. The voice came back, "If you are really the Son of God, why don't you jump and see if God sends the angels to catch you before you hit the stones below?"

Jesus said, "No. We do not need to test God."

Then, it was as if Jesus could see all the kingdoms of the world. The voice came back again: "If you will follow me, I will make you king over all these kingdoms."

MOVEMENTS

WORDS

Jesus said, "No. I am to be a king, but not that kind of king."

Then the voice went away.

Jesus went back across the Jordan and began to do his work. But what *was* his work?

Put the fourth plaque down on the fourth rectangle of the underlay.

⯈ Now I wonder what there is in this room that can help us tell more of this part of the story. Look around and see if you find something. I will go around the circle and invite each one of you to go and get something to put by this picture to help us show more of the story.

Begin to go around the circle, asking each child if he or she would like to bring something to put by the plaque illustrating "Jesus' Desert and Discovery Experience." Some children may not be able to think of anything, so move on if it looks as if they are stuck. You can come back to them later. If they are still stuck, that is okay. Many children learn by watching as well as by doing.

THE SECOND, THRI\IRD AND FOURTH PLAQUES ON THE UNDERLAY (STORYTELLER'S PERSPECTIVE)

Enjoy the items that the children bring to help tell the story. When you have had time to enjoy the entire layout, invite children, one at a time, to return their materials. Then take the plaques and underlay back to the Easter shelves.

Help the children begin to get out their work.

LESSON 6

THE FACES OF EASTER V

LESSON NOTES

FOCUS: JESUS AS HEALER AND PARABLE-MAKER

● LITURGICAL ACTION

● CORE PRESENTATION

THE MATERIAL

● LOCATION: EASTER SHELVES

● PIECES: SEVEN PLAQUES ILLUSTRATED WITH FACES OF CHRIST, WITH RACK

● UNDERLAY: PURPLE AND WHITE

BACKGROUND

Lent is the season when we prepare for Easter. This lesson continues to help children prepare for the Mystery of Easter. We move toward the Mystery by hearing the stories of Christ's journey toward the cross and resurrection. This week's presentation focuses on the face of Christ as healer and parable-maker.

You will begin this week's presentation by presenting a summary of the first four plaques:
• Jesus' Birth and Growth (pp. 32-36)
• Jesus Is Lost and Found (pp. 37-41)
• Jesus' Baptism and Blessing by God (pp. 42-46)
• Jesus' Desert and Discovery Experience (pp. 47-51)

Begin with those four presentations before adding the fifth plaque and its story.

NOTES ON THE MATERIAL

Find the materials for this presentation in the middle of the top shelf of the Easter shelves, in between the material for the Mystery of Easter, and the Synagogue and the Upper Room.

The material consists of a set of seven faces of Christ, mounted on wood or card-stock plaques. The underlay is a purple and white "scroll" that unrolls to show six purple rectangles and one white rectangle. Roll up the underlay so that the white rectangle is hidden inside.

A special carrier rack for the Faces plaques stands them up, making them visible to a child scanning the room full of materials. This stand for the plaques holds the rolled-up underlay. (See the illustration on p. 33.) If you do not use this stand, put the rolled-up underlay and plaques in a tray.

SPECIAL NOTES

Storytelling Tips: When Jerome Berryman first developed the presentations of the Faces of Christ, he thought it might be suitable only for older children. However, teachers at Christ Cathedral in Houston, who worked with these materials, used them with younger children, too—children as young as two years old. For the youngest children, keep the stories short, especially the summaries of previous stories. When you summarize the stories for very young children, you might only use a sentence or two for each story, for example:

• Here is the baby who was born.
• Here is the boy was lost and found.

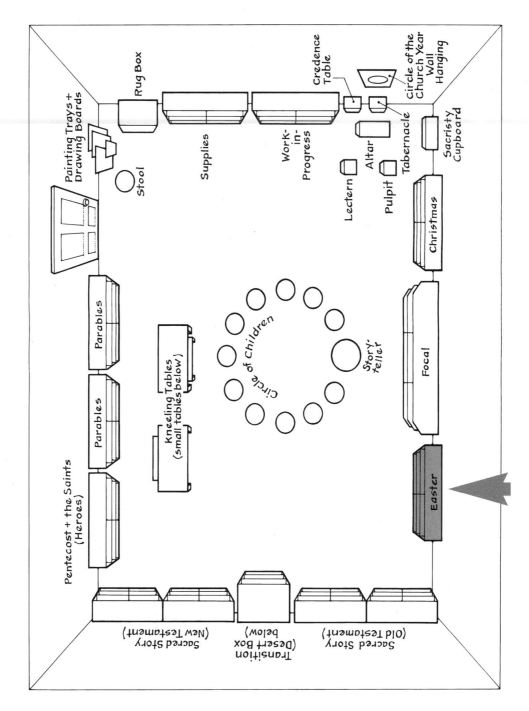

WHERE TO FIND MATERIALS

MOVEMENTS

When the children are ready, go to the Easter shelves and bring the plaques and rolled-up underlay to the circle.

Put the cards at your side and place the underlay in front of you. Unroll the underlay toward you to uncover the rectangle for the first plaque. Tell in summary the story "Jesus' Birth and Growth" (pp. 32-36). When you are finished, lay down the first plaque.

Unroll the underlay to uncover the rectangle for the second plaque. Tell in summary the story "Jesus Is Lost and Found" (pp. 37-41). When you are finished, lay down the second plaque.

Unroll the underlay to uncover the rectangle for the third plaque. Tell in summary the story "Jesus' Baptism and Blessing by God" (pp. 42-46). When you are finished, lay down the third plaque.

Unroll the underlay to uncover the rectangle for the fourth plaque. Tell in summary the story "Jesus' Desert and Discovery Experience" (pp. 47-51). When you are finished, lay down the fourth plaque.

Unroll the underlay to uncover the fifth rectangle. Pick up the fifth plaque and hold it so that the children can see it as you tell this story:

Point to the blind man.

WORDS

Watch carefully where I go so you will always know where to find this lesson.

Jesus came back across the Jordan River and began to do his work ...but what was his work? His work was to come close to people, especially the people no one else wanted to come close to.

See? He has come close to this blind man; he is so close that he has touched the blind man's eyes.

When Jesus came close to people, they changed. They could see things they could never see before. They could do things they could never do before. They became well.

MOVEMENTS

WORDS

Jesus also told parables. Finally, he knew that he had to become a parable, so he turned toward Jerusalem for the last time.

Put the fifth plaque down on the fifth rectangle of the underlay.

Now I wonder what there is in this room that can help us tell more of the story. Look around and see if you can bring something to show more about this part of the story. I will go around the circle and invite each one of you to go and get something to put by the picture to help us show more of the story.

Begin to go around the circle, asking each child if he or she would like to bring something to put by the plaque illustrating "Jesus as Healer and Parable-Maker." Some children may not be able to think of anything, so move on if it looks as if they are stuck. You can then come back to them later. If they are still stuck, that is okay. Many children learn by watching as well as by doing.

THE THIRD, FORTH AND FIFTH PLAQUES ON THE UNDERLAY (STORYTELLER'S PERSPECTIVE)

Enjoy the items that the children bring to help tell the story. When you have had time to enjoy the entire layout, invite children, one at a time, to return their materials. Then take the plaques and underlay back to the Easter shelves.

Help the children begin to get out their work.

THE FACES OF EASTER VI

LESSON NOTES

FOCUS: JESUS OFFERS THE BREAD AND WINE

● LITURGICAL ACTION

● CORE PRESENTATION

THE MATERIAL

● LOCATION: EASTER SHELVES

● PIECES: SEVEN PLAQUES ILLUSTRATED WITH FACES OF CHRIST, WITH RACK

● UNDERLAY: PURPLE AND WHITE

BACKGROUND

Lent is the season when we prepare for Easter. This lesson continues to help children prepare for the Mystery of Easter. We move toward the Mystery by hearing the stories of Christ's journey toward the cross and resurrection. This week's presentation focuses on the face of Christ as he enters Jerusalem and offers the Twelve—and us—the bread and wine.

You will begin this week's presentation by presenting a summary of the first five plaques:
• Jesus' Birth and Growth (pp. 32-36)
• Jesus Is Lost and Found (pp. 37-41)
• Jesus' Baptism and Blessing by God (pp. 42-46)
• Jesus' Desert and Discovery Experience (pp. 47-51)
• Jesus as Healer and Parable-Maker (pp. 52-56)

Begin with those five presentations before adding the sixth plaque and its story. If this is the last week you will meet before Easter, then tell the seventh Faces presentation (pp. 63-68), too.

NOTES ON THE MATERIAL

Find the materials for this presentation in the middle of the top shelf of the Easter shelves, in between the material for the Mystery of Easter, and the Synagogue and the Upper Room.

The material consists of a set of seven faces of Christ, mounted on wood or card-stock plaques. The underlay is a purple and white "scroll" that unrolls to show six purple rectangles and one white rectangle. Roll up the underlay so that the white rectangle is hidden inside.

A special carrier rack for the Faces plaques stands them up, making them visible to a child scanning the room full of materials. This stand for the plaques also holds the rolled-up underlay. If you do not use this stand, put the rolled-up underlay and plaques in a tray.

SPECIAL NOTES

At Home: When telling these stories in a home setting, remember to substitute "I wonder" questions for the activity of bringing other materials to place beside the plaques. Suitable "I wonder" questions for the last four Faces stories include:

- I wonder if anybody around this table has discovered who they are and what their work is going to be?
- I wonder if anyone in this family has come close to people—especially people no one else wanted to come close to? I wonder if anyone here has told parables? I wonder if anyone around this table has ever been sick?
- I wonder if anyone here has come close to holy bread and holy wine?
- I wonder if anyone here remembers their very best Easter? I wonder what the earliest Easter is you can remember?

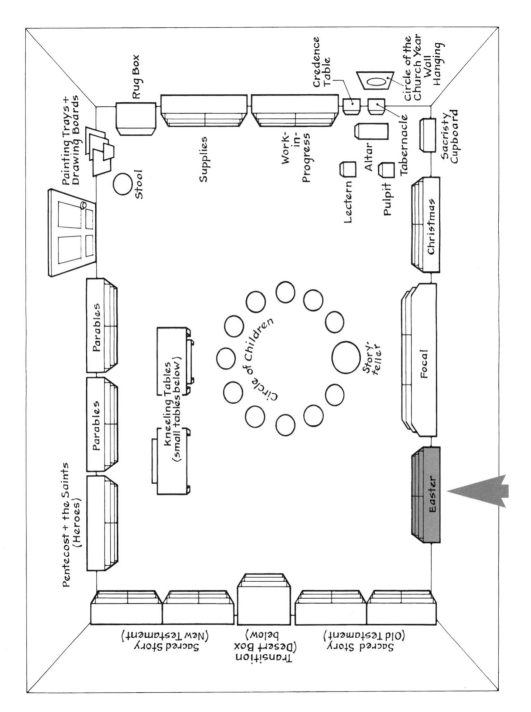

WHERE TO FIND MATERIALS

MOVEMENTS

When the children are ready, go to the Easter shelves. Bring the plaques and rolled-up underlay to the circle.

Put the cards at your side and place the underlay in front of you. Unroll the underlay toward you to uncover the rectangle for the first plaque. Tell in summary the story "Jesus' Birth and Growth" (pp. 32-36). When you are finished, lay down the first plaque.

Unroll the underlay to uncover the rectangle for the second plaque. Tell in summary the story of "Jesus Is Lost and Found" (pp. 37-41). When you are finished, lay down the second plaque.

Unroll the underlay to uncover the rectangle for the third plaque. Tell in summary the story "Jesus' Baptism and Blessing by God" (pp. 42-46). When you are finished, lay down the third plaque.

Unroll the underlay to uncover the rectangle for the fourth plaque. Tell in summary the story "Jesus' Desert and Discovery Experience" (pp. 47-51). When you are finished, lay down the fourth plaque.

Unroll the underlay to uncover the rectangle for the fifth plaque. Tell in summary the story "Jesus as Healer and Parable-Maker" (pp. 52-56). When you are finished, lay down the fifth plaque.

Unroll the underlay to uncover the sixth section. Pick up the sixth plaque and hold it so that the children can see it as you tell this story:

WORDS

➡ Watch carefully where I go so you will always know where to find this lesson.

➡ Jesus went to Jerusalem for the last time. It was the time of the Passover, and the city was full of people from many different lands. They thought Jesus was coming to be king, but they weren't paying attention.

He wasn't riding on a great white horse when he came into the city. He wasn't being carried by soldiers. He was riding on a donkey, and it wasn't even his. He had borrowed it.

MOVEMENTS	**WORDS**
	Still, that Sunday when Jesus came into Jerusalem, people waved palm branches, which were a sign of kings.

On Monday, Tuesday and Wednesday, Jesus went into the Temple to teach. Every night he went back to the Mount of Olives with the Twelve. The people watched him and whispered that the Mount of Olives was where angels were supposed to come down to make an army to drive away the Roman soldiers.

One day when Jesus was teaching in the Temple, he said, "Do you see that old woman over there? She's going to put something in the money box. Listen. Did you hear anything? No. She put the smallest coin there is in the box. That was all the money she had."

Now, here comes a rich man. He has so much money to put into the money box that he had to have help to carry it. His money makes a huge clanging and ringing as they pour it into the box.

Now, I wonder which one really gave the most, the old woman or the rich man.

Some said the rich man gave the most. Some said the old woman.

The Temple guards said, "On Thursday we will take him." But on Thursday, they could not find him. That evening, Jesus and the Twelve hurried through the dark streets to a house. They climbed up the stairs to an upper room and shared their last supper together.

After they had everything they wanted to eat, Jesus took some bread and gave thanks to God for it. Then he broke it and said something like, "Whenever you break the bread like this and share it, I will be there." He also took a cup of wine, gave thanks to God for it, and said, "Whenever you share a cup of wine like this, I will be there."

What was he talking about? He was always saying things like that. How could they know? Still, they did not forget, and later they would understand.

Suddenly Judas got up and left. The rest sang a hymn and then went to the Garden of Gethsemane on the Mount of Olives. Jesus wanted to pray. When he was finished, he joined the

MOVEMENTS

WORDS

Twelve, but Judas came out of the dark and greeted him. This was a signal for the Temple guards to take him. They too came out of the shadows and took Jesus away with them into the night. The Twelve disappeared into the darkness as well.

Put the sixth plaque down on the sixth rectangle of the underlay, with the face of Jesus toward the children.

Now I wonder what there is in this room that can help us tell more of this part of the story. Look around and see if you see something you can bring to put beside this picture. I will go around the circle and invite each one of you to go and get something to put by the picture to help us show more of the story.

Begin to go around the circle, asking each child if she or he would like to bring something to put by the plaque illustrating "Jesus Offers the Bread and Wine." Some children may not be able to think of anything, so move on if it looks as if they are stuck. You can come back to them later. If they are still stuck, that is okay. Many children learn by watching as well as by doing.

THE FOURTH, FIFTH AND SIXTH PLAQUES ON THE UNDERLAY (STORYTELLER'S PERSPECTIVE)

Enjoy the items that the children bring to help tell the story. When you have had time to enjoy the entire layout, invite children, one at a time, to return their materials. Then take the plaques and underlay back to the Easter shelves.

Help the children begin to get out their work.

THE FACES OF EASTER VII

LESSON NOTES

FOCUS: THE ONE WHO WAS EASTER AND STILL IS

● LITURGICAL ACTION

● CORE PRESENTATION

THE MATERIAL

● LOCATION: EASTER SHELVES

● PIECES: SEVEN PLAQUES ILLUSTRATED WITH FACES OF CHRIST, WITH RACK

● UNDERLAY: PURPLE AND WHITE

BACKGROUND

Lent is the season when we prepare for Easter. This lesson continues to help children prepare for the Mystery of Easter. We move toward the Mystery by hearing the stories of Christ's journey toward the cross and resurrection. This last presentation focuses on the faces of Christ on the cross and on Easter.

You will begin this week's presentation by presenting a summary of the first six plaques:
• Jesus' Birth and Growth (pp. 32-36)
• Jesus Is Lost and Found (pp. 37-41)
• Jesus' Baptism and Blessing by God (pp. 42-46)
• Jesus' Desert and Discovery Experience (pp. 47-51)
• Jesus as Healer and Parable-Maker (pp. 52-56)
• Jesus Offers the Bread and Wine (pp. 57-62)

Begin with those six presentations before adding the last plaque and its story.

NOTES ON THE MATERIAL

Find the materials for this presentation in the middle of the top shelf of the Easter shelves, in between the material for the Mystery of Easter and the Synagogue and the Upper Room.

The material consists of a set of seven faces of Christ, mounted on wood or card-stock plaques. The underlay is a purple and white "scroll" that unrolls to show six purple rectangles and one white rectangle. Roll up the underlay so that the white rectangle is hidden inside.

A special carrier rack for the Faces plaques stands them up, making them visible to a child scanning the room full of materials. This stand for the plaques should also hold the rolled-up underlay. (See the illustration on p. 33.) If you do not use this stand, put the rolled-up underlay and plaques in a tray.

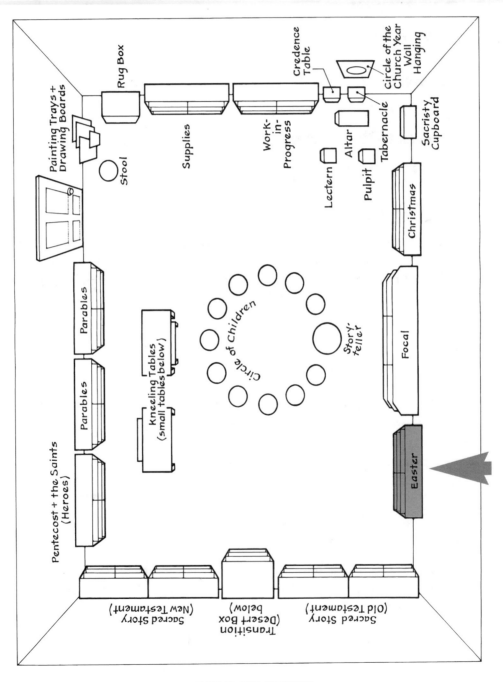

WHERE TO FIND MATERIALS

MOVEMENTS

When the children are ready, go to the Easter shelves and bring the plaques and rolled-up underlay to the circle.

Put the cards at your side and place the underlay in front of you. Unroll the underlay toward you to uncover the rectangle for the first plaque. Tell in summary the story "Jesus' Birth and Growth" (pp. 32-36). When you are finished, lay down the first plaque.

Unroll the underlay to uncover the rectangle for the second plaque. Tell in summary the story "Jesus Is Lost and Found" (pp. 37-41). When you are finished, lay down the second plaque.

Unroll the underlay to uncover the rectangle for the third plaque. Tell in summary the story "Jesus' Baptism and Blessing by God" (pp. 42-46). When you are finished, lay down the third plaque.

Unroll the underlay to uncover the rectangle for the fourth plaque. Tell in summary the story "Jesus' Desert and Discovery Experience" (pp. 47-51). When you are finished, lay down the fourth plaque.

Unroll the underlay to uncover the rectangle for the fifth plaque. Tell in summary the story "Jesus as Healer and Parable-Maker" (pp. 52-56). When you are finished, lay down the fifth plaque.

Unroll the underlay to uncover the rectangle for the sixth plaque. Tell in summary the story "Jesus Offers the Bread and Wine" (pp. 57-62). When you are finished, lay down the sixth plaque.

WORDS

⏵ Watch carefully where I go so you will always know where to find this lesson.

MOVEMENTS

Don't unroll the seventh section of the underlay yet. Pick up the seventh plaque and hold it, with the face of Christ on the Cross facing the children. Tell this story:

Point to the dark sky.

Turn the plaque slowly back and forth as you describe the Faces in this part of the story, showing first one side, then the other. Finally, turn the edge of the plaque toward the children and "try" to pull the two sides apart.

Now unroll the white rectangle of the underlay.

Put the seventh plaque down on the white rectangle, with the face of the Risen Christ facing up.

WORDS

The night was a confusing one. The next day, Jesus was taken outside the walls of the city and crucified.

That afternoon, Jesus died. The sky grew dark. Jesus was taken down from the cross and buried in a cave. A great stone was rolled into the opening of the cave to close it like a door.

Saturday was so quiet you could almost hear the earth breathing. On Sunday, it was the women who had the courage to go to the tomb just to be close to Jesus. They wanted to remember, even if it was sad. When they came to the tomb, they found that the stone had been rolled back and that the tomb was empty.

Jesus had died on the cross, but somehow he was still with them as he is with us, especially in the bread and the wine.

When you look at this side (crucifixion), you know that the other side is there (Easter). When you look at this side (Easter), you know that this side (crucifixion) is there, and you cannot pull them apart. This is the Mystery of Easter, and that makes all the difference...

...and so the colors change.

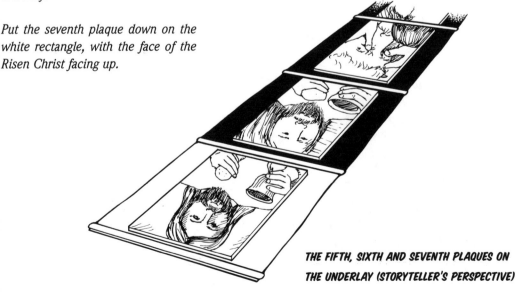

THE FIFTH, SIXTH AND SEVENTH PLAQUES ON THE UNDERLAY (STORYTELLER'S PERSPECTIVE)

MOVEMENTS

WORDS

Sit back and enjoy the complete story laid out in a line, then look puzzled. Say:

⇒ Wait a minute. There's something wrong.

Point to each part as you call attention to the linear layout of the story.

⇒ Here's the beginning...the middle...and the end.

Pick up the seventh plaque and turn it to the crucifixion side.

⇒ Look! If we have only this side, the story has an end...

Turn the plaque over to the Easter side and show it to the children.

⇒ ...but there is also this side.

Put the Easter plaque back on the white panel, resurrection side up.

⇒ The ending is also a beginning, so we can't leave the story in a line.

Pick up the first plaque and roll the underlay toward you out of the way. Place the first plaque down where the first portion of the underlay was.

⇒ Let's see what we can do.

Pick up the second plaque and roll up the second section of the underlay. Place the second plaque where indicated in the illustration on the next page.

Pick up the third plaque and roll up the third section of the underlay. Place the third plaque where indicated in the illustration.

Pick up the fourth plaque and roll up the fourth section of the underlay. Place the fourth plaque where indicated in the illustration.

Pick up the fifth plaque and roll up the fifth section of the underlay. Place the fifth plaque where indicated in the illustration.

Pick up the sixth plaque and roll up the sixth section of the underlay. Place the sixth plaque where indicated in the illustration.

I wonder

MOVEMENTS

Finally, pick up the seventh plaque and hold it while you finish rolling up the underlay. Place the underlay beside you. Place the seventh plaque (resurrection-side up) in the middle of the layout where indicated in the illustration.

WORDS

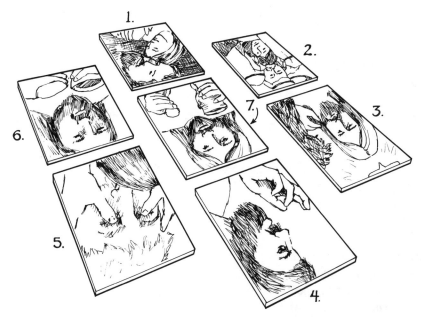

THE CIRCLE OF FACES (STORYTELLER'S PERSPECTIVE)

Say:

⇒ Now the story can go on forever.

I wonder what part of this story you like best?

I wonder what part of the story is the most important part?

I wonder where you are in this story? What part of the story is about you?

I wonder if there is any part of the story we can leave out and still have all the story we need.

When the energy in the wondering begins to wane, help the children to make choices about the work they are going to get out.

THE CROSSES

LESSON NOTES

FOCUS: EXPLORING A SACRED SYMBOL

● LITURGICAL ACTION

● ENRICHMENT PRESENTATION

THE MATERIAL

● LOCATION: EASTER SHELVES

● PIECES: COLLECTION OF CROSSES IN A CONTAINER; OPTIONAL: CARDS TO NAME AND EXPLAIN THE CROSSES

● UNDERLAY: NONE (USE A RUG.)

BACKGROUND

Save this lesson for the time when a child decides to "make a cross" for his or her art response. It's great fun to hold this in reserve for such an occasion, because when a child says, "I'm going to make a cross," you can say, "Which one?" The teachable moment has arrived!

This lesson is also useful when a child cannot think of anything at all to make, even "a cross." You can get the basket of crosses and begin to wonder with him or her about what they all mean and who first made them. This can lead to the child making a cross that is just right for his or her life.

The cross lesson can be started quickly and put away quickly. It can take as long as the child wants to work on it. You can present this to an individual child, without introducing it through a group lesson.

NOTES ON THE MATERIAL

Find the materials for this presentation on the right-hand side of the bottom shelf of the Easter shelves, underneath the material for the Easter Egg presentation.

There are several ways to make this material. You could simply put all the three-dimensional, wooden crosses you collect into a basket and place it on the shelf. You could also draw or mount cross shapes on cards or wooden plaques, and create an additional set of cards with stories or explanations about each cross.

The best material combines the two approaches. In a beautiful container, place a set of wooden cross shapes. Make a set of cards with the names of each cross shape and an explanation of that shape to serve as identification and control cards for the children. (Control cards help children sort the material and make sure each item is present and named.) The collection offered through Godly Play Resources includes a Greek cross, a Latin cross, a Celtic cross, a budded cross, a St. Andrew's cross, an Egyptian (or Coptic) cross and an anchor cross.

SPECIAL NOTES

Classroom Management: Sometimes children make crosses because they can't think of anything else to make. If so, they might not go very deeply into the activity, because they are doing it for you and not out of personal interest. This lesson challenges them to think about what crosses really represent and how to work with crosses to find the cross that is just right for them. This can reveal important things about who they are or hope to be.

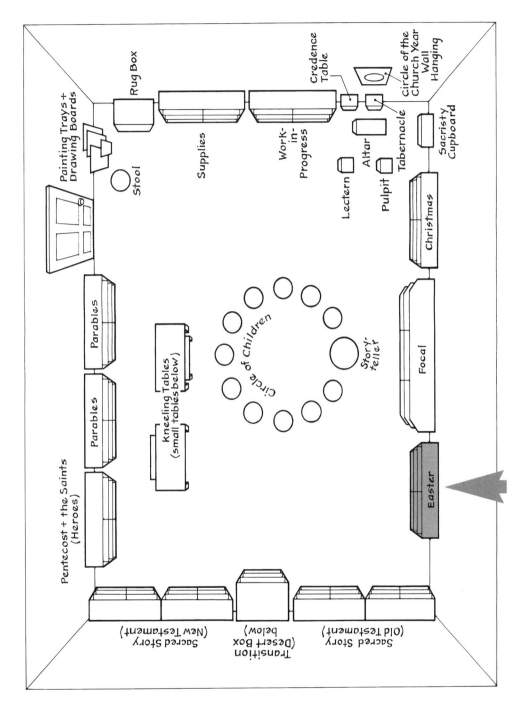

WHERE TO FIND MATERIALS

MOVEMENTS

When children cannot decide what to do, or when they say they are going to "make a cross," you can challenge them to discover more about crosses and about themselves.

Don't say too much about where the crosses in the classroom or the container of crosses might be. This can help a child or group search the room and become more familiar with all the materials that are there waiting for them to work with. As the children look, go and get a rug. Spread it out in just the right place. Then, if necessary, go find the basket of crosses.

Bring the basket back to the rug. Take out the crosses and line them up on the rug.

If there is a set of cards to use as a control, you can explain them to the children. Show the pictures of the crosses and the names for and explanations about them. Read them for the nonreaders.

WORDS

➡ Oh, so you would like to make a cross? That will be wonderful work. Let's see now...which one are you going to make? There are so many kinds! How many? Oh, I don't know, but we have at least a dozen in our classroom. Why don't you see if you can find them? The cross has a lot to do with the Mystery of Easter.

➡ Look at all these crosses. Do you see the differences between them? Each one has a name and a story. Is one of these just right for you? Would you like to make one? Which one will it be? What will you make it out of? Do you want to draw or paint them? Can you make one that is different from any in the basket? Maybe there is not one that is just right for you.

➡ These cards are for you. You can use them when you have questions or are naming the crosses.

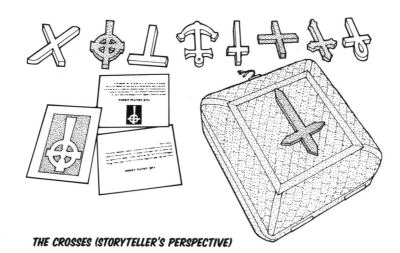

THE CROSSES (STORYTELLER'S PERSPECTIVE)

MOVEMENTS

Begin the wondering questions.

Put the crosses back into the container for the children to work with. As you put them back, hold them carefully and with respect. Don't hurry. Name each cross with wonder as you replace it.

WORDS

 Now I wonder which cross you like best?

I wonder which is the most important cross?

I wonder which cross is especially for you?

I wonder if we can leave out any of these crosses and still have all the crosses we need?

Now I wonder if you would like to make something about how these crosses feel to you?

ENRICHMENT LESSON
EASTER EGGS

LESSON NOTES

FOCUS: SYMBOLS OF THE MYSTERY OF EASTER

- LITURGICAL ACTION
- ENRICHMENT PRESENTATION

THE MATERIAL

- LOCATION: EASTER SHELVES
- PIECES: I TRAY-SHAPED BASKET; I SQUARE BASKET HOLDING I-3 UKRAINIAN EASTER EGGS IN TRANSLUCENT BOXES; I REAL (OR WOODEN) EGG IN A SMALL BASKET COVERED WITH A WHITE CLOTH; COLLECTION OF TWO-DIMENSIONAL, EGG-SHAPED SAMPLES OF COLORS, DESIGNS AND FINISHED PATTERNS; OPTIONAL: PAPER, PLAIN EGGS (WOODEN OR REAL), EASTER "GRASS" AND SMALL BASKETS FOR THE CHILDREN
- UNDERLAY: NONE (USE A RUG.)

BACKGROUND

The folk celebration of Easter eggs brings delight at this time of year. Our culture's Easter eggs have little to do with the Easter that is celebrated in churches, but the eggs of Eastern Europe do. Introducing children to these eggs is a way to reclaim a wonderful sign of new life in Easter for children.

One never knows what the creativity of children will teach us. Children sometimes enjoy transferring the lesson about Easter eggs to Advent. They make "Christmas eggs" to give as presents at Christmas time. They are covered with the symbols of the Mystery of Christmas instead of Easter.

NOTES ON THE MATERIAL

Find the materials for this presentation on the right-hand side of the middle shelf of the Easter shelves, underneath the material for the Synagogue and the Upper Room.

This material fits onto one large basket, about 1' x 2'. Inside the large basket are three additional baskets:

- One square basket (8" x 8") holds up to three Ukrainian Easter eggs in translucent boxes with lids.
- Another square basket (6" x 6") is covered by a white cloth. *Before beginning the presentation, take one of the Ukrainian Easter eggs out of its translucent box and place it in this basket.*
- An oval basket holds a collection of flat, egg-shaped wood or cardboard samples showing some of the traditional colors and patterns used in making Ukrainian Easter eggs.

MEANING OF THE TRADITIONAL COLORS

white	purity
yellow	spirituality
blue	health
pink	success
black	remembrance
orange	attraction
brown	happiness
green	money
purple	high power
red	love

There is also a collection of flat, egg-shaped wood or cardboard samples showing some of the traditional design elements used.

MEANING OF THE TRADITIONAL DESIGN ELEMENTS

butterfly	nature
flower	love, charity
circle, poppy, spider web	the sun, good fortune
checkerboard, sieve	filtering good from evil
ladders	growing, climbing to heaven
fish	ancient Christian symbol
bends, spirals	Life doesn't always go in "straight lines."
deer, horses	prosperity, wealth
wheat	bountiful harvest
hens, roosters, sparrows, storks	wishes coming true (The birds are always resting.)
star	rose
cross	suffering, death, resurrection of Christ
ram's horns	strength, determination
eight-pointed star	About the year 988 this sign of the sun god became a symbol for the Christian God.
pine trees, needles	eternal youth and health
dots	stars in heaven, Mary's tears
designs encircling the egg	eternity

OTHER DESIGN ELEMENTS, MEANING UNKNOWN

spoons, leaves	Spoons stand alone. Leaves come in two and threes.
rake	for sorting and for planting

Finally, there is a collection of additional finished eggs with various degrees of complexity.

SAMPLE EGG PATTERNS AND DESIGNS

For children to make their own projects, you'll need sheets of drawing paper. You can add plain wooden eggs or blown, fresh eggs for the children to decorate with art supplies, too.

SPECIAL NOTES

Storytelling Tip: The Ukrainian eggs in the translucent boxes are real and fragile. If one gets broken, leave it in its box so the children can see for themselves how thin the shells are.

A wonderful children's book that shows real children making real Ukrainian Easter eggs is *A Kid's Guide to Decorating Ukrainian Easter Eggs* by Natalie Perchyshyn, published by and available from the Ukrainian Gift Shop, 1-612-788-2545, or: *www.ukrainiangiftshop.com*

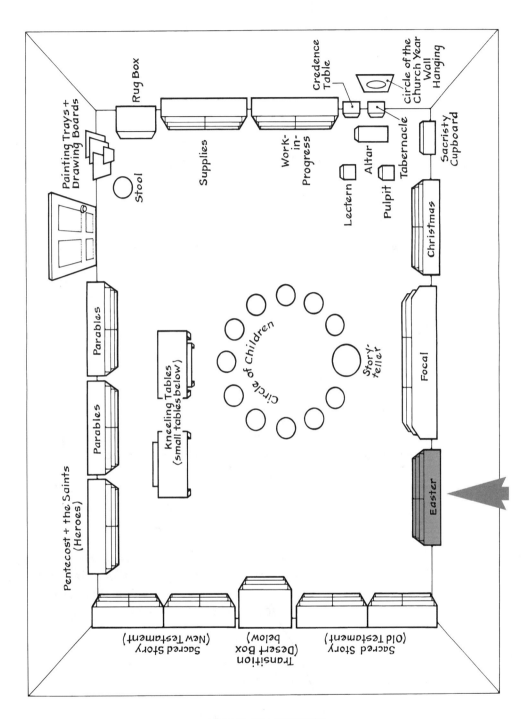

WHERE TO FIND MATERIALS

MOVEMENTS

Go to the rug box and get a rug. Unroll it in front of you.

Go to the shelves and find the materials for the Easter Eggs lesson. Place the materials beside you. When you and the children are settled, begin.

In the middle of the circle, place the 6" x 6" basket containing a single Ukrainian Easter egg. (You prepared this before the session.) Hold the white, real (or wooden) egg hidden in your closed hand.

Turn your hand over and show the children the white egg. Put the egg in the basket. As you do so, keep the Ukrainian egg hidden under the cover.

WORDS

Watch carefully where I go so you will always know where to find this lesson.

We are coming close to the Mystery of Easter. There are all kinds of ways to get ready to come close to this great mystery. Some are done in the church, and some are done outside the church. One of the things done outside of the church is to make Easter eggs. The only trouble is that many people have forgotten how to make real Easter eggs. They don't even know their story. Let me tell you the story

There was once an old man and an old woman who lived just outside the walls of the great city of Jerusalem. They had everything they needed. They had a cow to give them milk. They had a garden to give them vegetables. They had trees to give them apples, figs and dates. They had chickens to give them eggs.

In the morning the old man would go out to the hen house and say to the hens, "Good morning. May I have some of your eggs?" They gladly gave him their eggs, and there were plenty. There were so many on some days that the old man took the ones they did not eat into the city to sell.

One day he went into the great city of Jerusalem with a basket full of eggs. A white cloth covered them. He went in through the high gate and went along a narrow stone street. As he came closer to one of the wide streets, there was a huge crowd. They were strangely quiet. He pushed his way through the crowd with his basket of eggs to see what was going on.

The Roman soldiers were taking three people through the city to crucify them outside the city walls. They were carrying the crosses they were to be nailed to. One of them stumbled and almost fell as the old man watched.

He couldn't help it. He stepped out from the crowd and caught the heavy, wooden beam before the man fell. Together they carried the piece of wood outside the walls.

The old man stayed there all afternoon. Even when the sky grew dark and it began to rain, he stayed there. He watched the mother and others standing there. They were watching the man in the middle. Finally, he died.

MOVEMENTS

WORDS

They took the man down and carried him away to put in a stone tomb. The old man did not follow. He started back towards the city. As he went in through the sad gate, he suddenly remembered his eggs. Where were they?

He hurried back to the basket. Then he remembered. He had quickly put the basket down to help. How could they be there? Too many people were hungry, and eggs were precious even to people who were not hungry.

He turned the corner, and like a joke, looked at the place he had put down the basket. It was there! He rubbed his eyes. He looked again. Yes. It was really there.

He looked in the basket. The white covering was still there, but he knew the eggs underneath would be gone. He reached under the white cover. There was something there.

Take out the colored egg. ⟶ When he pulled out one of the eggs, he could not believe his eyes. It was like a jewel!

Pick up the basket so the children can't see inside. ⟶ The old man picked up the basket and pulled back the cover. The basket was full of beautiful eggs. They were covered with colors and designs. The eggs were trying to say with colors and lines what had happened that day!

When the old man told this story, people began to color eggs at Eastertime, and they still do to this very day. Some don't even know why, but you do.

When the story is finished, return the Ukrainian egg you've been using to its box and take out the other Ukrainian eggs. Place all three eggs, in their boxes, on the rug. Show the eggs to the children.

Show children the samples of finished designs.

MOVEMENTS

WORDS

Show children the egg shapes with samples of traditional colors and design elements. Lay them out in lines as you describe them.

Here are shapes of eggs you can trace to fill in with your own design. Here are colors and designs that other people have used, but there is no one else in the world who knows what your egg is supposed to look like. Only you can decide.

Fold an 8-1/2" x 11" sheet of paper in half and then fold that half in half again to make a booklet.

Here is how you can make a booklet about your egg.

Trace an egg design on the front of the cover.

On the cover of your booklet, you can draw an egg shape.

Decorate your drawing of an egg. Look up what everything means. Write that on the inside of your booklet. If you are not a reader and writer yet, ask someone to write it out for you.

If you are planning to have children decorate real eggs, either wooden or fresh, you can say:

When you are finished with the booklet, you can then decorate an egg.

If you are supplying wooden eggs, you can say:

These eggs were not laid by chickens, but they are "forest fresh." They come from trees.

When the egg is finished, we will put it in a basket with grass, so you can give it to anyone, even to yourself.

Begin the wondering questions.

Now I wonder which of the colors and designs you like best?

I wonder which colors and designs are the most important?

I wonder which colors and designs are especially about you?

I wonder if these are all the designs and colors we need? Maybe we need more? Are there too many? Not enough?

After the wondering, carefully replace the materials and return the basket to its shelf.

Now watch carefully where I go, so you will always be able to find this work.

Help the children choose their work.

LESSON 9
JESUS AND THE TWELVE

LESSON NOTES
FOCUS: THE TWELVE APOSTLES

- **SACRED STORY**
- **CORE PRESENTATION**

THE MATERIAL

- **LOCATION: SACRED STORY (NEW TESTAMENT) SHELVES**
- **PIECES: PICTURE OF LAST SUPPER, SYMBOLS FOR THE 12 APOSTLES, CONTROL CARD(S)**
- **UNDERLAY: NONE**

BACKGROUND

The word *apostle* is a transliteration of the Greek word, *apostos*. While the term *apostle* suggests one who proclaims the faith, the term *disciple* suggests being a student of a religious leader. The title *apostle* is applied to Matthias, Barnabas and Paul. Matthias took Judas' place, but neither Barnabas nor Paul was one of the Twelve. Sometimes the word *apostle* is used to designate the leader of the first Christian mission to a country. For example, Patrick is called "the apostle of Ireland" and Augustine of Canterbury is called "the apostle of England." Technically, then, the Twelve were disciples until they began to proclaim the faith on their own; then they became apostles. As we look back from the perspective of today, however, we acknowledge that they did eventually share their own faith, so we call them "apostles."

There are four lists of the apostles in the New Testament, found in Matthew 10:2-4, Mark 3:16-19, Luke 6:14-16 and Acts 1:13. The four lists give contradictory names for the Twelve. This historical difficulty has several scholarly solutions, but our pedagogical purpose is to present the group as the Twelve, with a fixed set of names.

We will use this list, based on the traditional names for the Twelve, together with their traditional symbols:

Name	*Symbol*
Andrew	white X-shaped cross on blue background
Bartholomew	three knives
James (son of Zebedee)	three scallop shells and often a sword

Name	Symbol
James the Less (son of Alphaeus)	saw
John	cup and serpent
Jude	sailboat
Matthew	three money bags
Philip	cross with two loaves of bread
Thomas	builder's square and spear
Simon Peter	upside-down cross and crossed keys
Simon, the Zealot	book and fish

Those are eleven apostles. Judas, the twelfth apostle, removed himself from the Twelve through his betrayal and suicide. The twelfth shield is for Matthias, who replaced Judas after Jesus' ascension into heaven. His symbol is the sword and a book.

NOTES ON THE MATERIAL

Find the materials for this presentation on the top shelf of the sacred story shelves. A reproduction of Da Vinci's *The Last Supper* leans against the wall in the New Testament section. In front of the painting, there should be a tray holding a small basket containing twelve small shields and control cards (described below).

The reproduction of the Last Supper can be mounted on foamcore. The moment Da Vinci depicts is the reaction of the disciples to Christ's statement that "One of you will betray me." Christ has one palm turned down, as if to say, "If it be possible, let this cup pass from me." The other palm is turned up, as if to say, "Not my will but thine be done."

Some historical notes on the painting, which you may want to discuss with older children:
- The people are dressed in the clothes of the painter's time and place. They are late 15th century, north Italian and wealthy. The painting was painted about the time Columbus discovered America.
- They look like someone who might buy a painting from Da Vinci.
- A more important cultural issue is the painting's display of anti-Semitism. The only person who looks "Jewish," dark with curly hair, is Judas. Children will remind you that they have Jewish friends, however, who don't look like that. For his time, Da Vinci painted a representative figure, a stereotype.

As you tell the story, you will place each shield above the head of the matching apostle. A control card shows the name of each apostle in Da Vinci's picture. Other cards could show pictures of the shields with the names of the matching apostles. You can buy a set of these cards from Godly Play Resources or make them yourself.

MATCHING SHIELDS TO APOSTLES (STORYTELLER'S PERSPECTIVE)

SPECIAL NOTES

Storytelling Tip: In telling this story, you can change the order of presenting the Twelve from the one we give in order to tell the stories of those apostles whose symbols and stories you remember first, hoping the others will come to mind as you proceed! The lesson uses the four groupings of three apostles as suggested by the Da Vinci painting.

Additional significant groupings are:
- two sets of brothers: Peter and Andrew, James and John (sons of Zebedee)
- the inner circle, present at the Transfiguration: Peter, James and John
- one set of friends: Philip and Bartholomew
- those directly called by Jesus: Philip and Matthew
- the only one to die a natural death: John

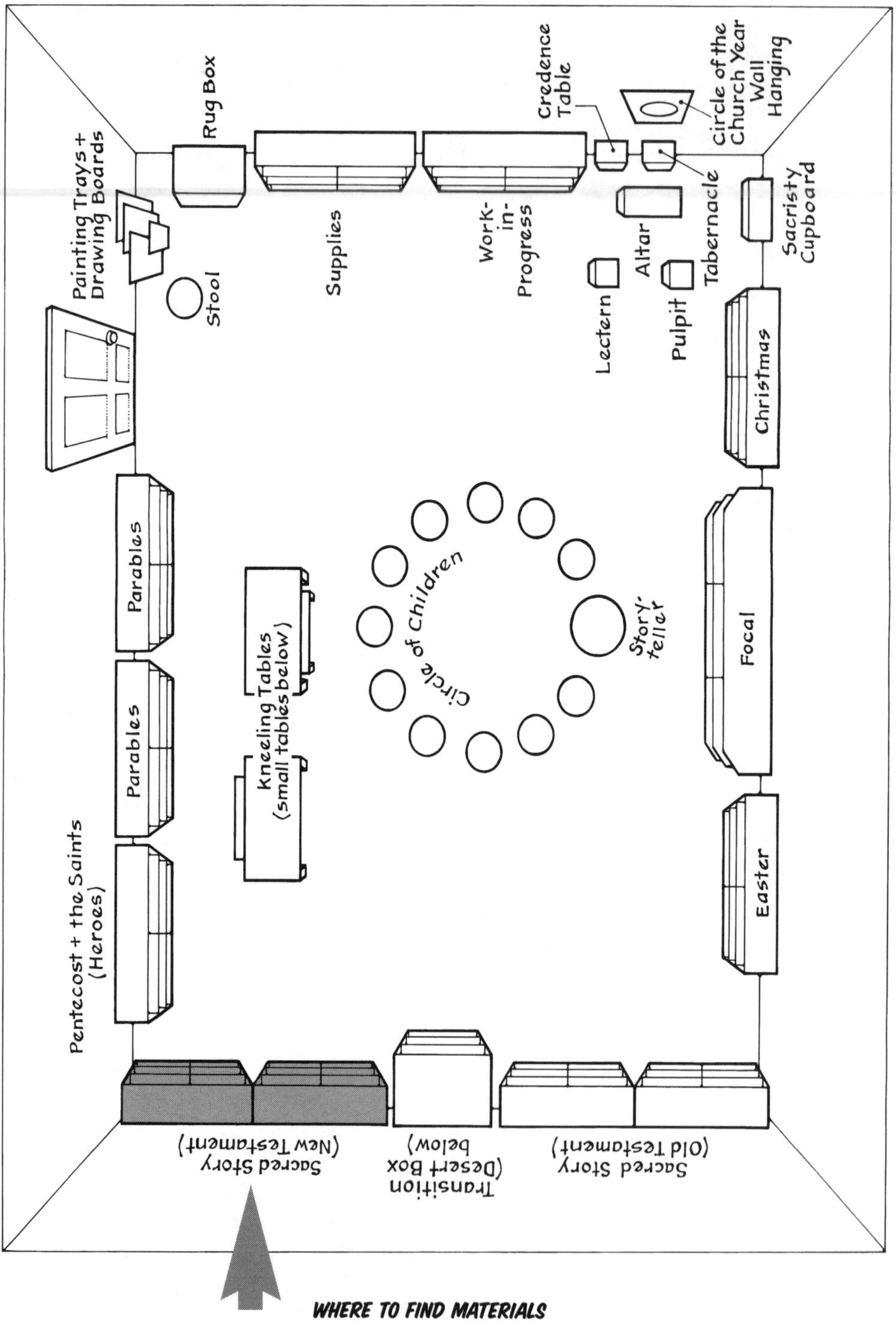

Rug Box
Painting Trays + Drawing Boards
Stool
Supplies
Work-in-Progress
Credence Table
Circle of the Church Year Wall Hanging
Tabernacle
Altar
Lectern
Pulpit
Sacristy Cupboard
Christmas
Focal
Easter
Parables
Parables
Pentecost + the Saints (Heroes)
Kneeling Tables (small tables below)
Circle of Children
Story-teller
Sacred Story (New Testament)
Transition (Desert Box below)
Sacred Story (Old Testament)

WHERE TO FIND MATERIALS

MOVEMENTS	WORDS
When the children are ready, bring the picture and tray of materials to the circle. Put the tray beside you. Put the picture in front of you, facing away from you. As you tell this story, you can tilt the picture up, laying it against your knees to help the children see it more clearly.	⇒ Watch carefully where I go so you will always know where to find this lesson.
Sweep your hand over the picture as you name the Twelve.	⇒ When Jesus went to Jerusalem for the last time, he went with the Twelve. They were his special friends. Today we call them the apostles.
Point to some of the bread and wine on the table when you name them.	⇒ On Thursday of the last week, they met in an upstairs room for their last meal together. It was when Jesus told them that he would always be with them—and us—when we share the holy bread and wine. But something happened just before he shared the holy bread and wine with them.
Point to Jesus.	⇒ Jesus said, "Someone who is sitting at this table will betray me."
Sweep your hand over the apostles again.	⇒ All the apostles were shocked and sorry and angry. They cried out, "Is it I?" "Who is it?" That is what you see happening in the painting.
Point to Judas.	⇒ Later, Judas did betray Jesus. He showed the High Priest's soldiers who Jesus was that night in the Garden of Gethsemane.
Take the shields from their container and lay them out across the top of the picture in random order.	⇒ These are the symbols of the apostles. Each one has a special sign to help us remember them and their stories.
Use your finger to draw an imaginary circle around each one of the groups.	⇒ Jesus is in the middle. The apostles are in groups of three on either side. Let's see who's here.
Point to John. With the picture facing away from you toward the children, John is seated directly to your right of Jesus.	⇒ This is John. He is probably the one called the "beloved disciple." John first learned about Jesus when he was with John the Baptist. Right away he told his brother, James, and they both began to follow Jesus. Both brothers were fishermen. Their father's name was Zebedee. John is probably the one who wrote down the story of Jesus we call "The Gospel of John."

MOVEMENTS

Move the shield for John down from the row of shields along the top of the picture so that it rests right over his head.

Lean back and pause each time before moving on to the next apostle. Now point to Peter. With the picture facing away from you toward the children, Peter is seated directly to the right of John, two places to the right from Jesus and behind Judas as you look at the picture.

Move the shield for Peter down from the row of shields along the top of the picture so that it rests right over his head.

Point to Judas. With the picture facing away from you toward the children, Judas is seated to the right and in front of Peter, three places to the right of Jesus.

Make a motion as if moving a shield for Judas down over his head, but with no shield: there is no symbol for Judas.

Move the shield for Matthias down from the row of shields along the top of the picture, over the head of Judas.

WORDS

This is the symbol for John. On his shield are the cup and the snake. They help us remember how one time some people tried to put poison into his cup, but the snake came and drank it. The snake died to save John's life.

Stories say that John was the only apostle who was not killed. He died on an island when he was an old man, full of years.

This is Peter. He is leaning in toward Jesus behind Judas. Peter often got angry. He looks angry now, but he became more peaceful as the years went by.

Peter heard about Jesus from his brother, Andrew, who was with John the Baptist. He is sitting next to his brother, but it is hard to tell because of the way he is leaning in towards John. The two brothers look a lot alike.

Peter's sign is the crossed keys and an upside-down cross. One time Jesus said to Peter that he was the rock on which he would build the church. He then said that he gave Peter the keys to the kingdom.

When Peter was old, he went to be with the Christian people in Rome. It was against the law to be a Christian person in those days, and the soldiers caught him. When they were going to nail him to a cross like Jesus, Peter asked them to turn him upside down. He did not deserve to die like his Lord, he said. The soldiers did as he asked, and old Peter died on the cross, too, but upside down.

Judas is the one who went against Jesus. See? He is holding a bag with thirty pieces of silver in it. That is what he was paid to show the soldiers who Jesus was when they went to arrest him in the Garden of Gethsemane.

Sometimes the sign for Judas is a shield that is all black. Sometimes it has the thirty pieces of silver or a rope on it. I wonder if that is completely true. I wonder if Jesus forgave him.

This is the sign for Matthias. He replaced Judas as one of the Twelve.

MOVEMENTS	WORDS
Draw an imaginary circle around the next group of three, the three closest to the other side of Jesus.	On the other side of Jesus are Thomas, James and Philip.
Point to Thomas. With the picture facing away from you toward the children, Thomas is seated to the left of Jesus, behind James.	This is Thomas. He is leaning behind James, so we see his face next to Jesus, even though James is really sitting next to Jesus. Thomas was the one who always asked hard questions. He is sometimes called "doubting Thomas."
Move the shield for Thomas down from the row of shields along the top of the picture so that it rests right over his head.	His sign is a spear and a builder's square. This is what a builder uses to make square corners on buildings. Thomas went to India to tell people the story of Jesus, so he began to build the Church in that part of the world. He was killed in India for telling the story.
Point to James. With the picture facing away from you toward the children, James is seated to the left of Jesus, in front of Thomas. Show how James is really sitting next to Jesus, even though the face of Thomas is closer to Jesus.	This is James. He is really sitting next to Jesus. His brother, John, is on one side, and he is on the other. He and his brother were fishermen, like Peter and Andrew. They worked for their father, Zebedee. James learned about Jesus from his brother, John, who learned about him when he was a disciple of John the Baptist. The two brothers, John and James, together with Peter, made up an inner circle of three very close friends of Jesus inside the group of the Twelve. The three were there when Jesus was praying on the mountain and when he was praying in the garden, but I'm afraid they went to sleep three times in the garden.
Move the shield for James down from the row of shields along the top of the picture so that it rests right over his head.	The sign of James is three shells. He was the first apostle to be killed. King Herod Agrippa I had him executed. This is why a sword is also sometimes on his symbol.
Point to Philip. With the picture facing away from you toward the children, Philip is seated to the left of James, three places to the left of Jesus. Trace how Philip is leaning in toward Jesus.	Philip is next. He was there when Jesus fed 5,000 people. They were hungry for the truth about life, and Jesus told them. The truth is that people need each other and need to love each other. Jesus shared a little bread and fish with all those people to show this in a way so they could understand and yet keep thinking about. Jesus was like that.
Move the shield for Philip down from the row of shields along the top of the picture so that it rests right over his head.	His sign has two loaves of bread on it to remember that day when so many were fed with the bread of truth.

MOVEMENTS	WORDS
Move your finger across to the other end of the table, the right side of the table with the picture facing away from you toward the children. Then circle the group of three disciples there.	Now we will go back to the other side, clear to the end of the table. Here there is another group of three people. They are Andrew, James the Less and Bartholomew.
Point to Andrew. With the picture facing away from you toward the children, Andrew is seated to the right of Judas, four places to the right of Jesus (from the storyteller's perspective).	Here is Andrew. We already know he is Peter's brother. See how he is sitting near to Peter? Andrew was one of John the Baptist's disciples, but when John the Baptist showed Jesus to him, he went to get his brother Peter, and they both followed Jesus. Both Andrew and Peter were fishermen.
Move the shield for Andrew down from the row of shields along the top of the picture so that it rests right over his head.	Many centuries ago the people of Scotland liked Andrew so much that they made him the patron saint of Scotland. If you should ever go there, you will still see his sign, the cross that looks like an "X" with a blue background. He died on a cross that was this shape.
Point to James the Less. With the picture facing away from you toward the children, James the Less is seated to the right of Andrew, five places to the right of Jesus.	James the Less is next. People called him "the Less" because he was younger or shorter than John's brother James.
Move the shield for James the Less down from the row of shields along the top of the picture so that it rests right over his head.	James the Less's sign is a saw. He was killed by a saw for telling the story of Jesus. Kings did not like to hear about following "a king" called Jesus, even though Jesus was a different kind of king.
Point to Bartholomew. With the picture facing away from you toward the children, Bartholomew is seated at the farthest right of the table.	Finally at this end of the table we come to Bartholomew. His name means "Son of Tolmai." He was told about Jesus by Philip after Jesus told Philip to follow him.
Move the shield for Bartholomew down from the row of shields along the top of the picture so that it rests right over his head.	This is Bartholomew's sign. He was killed by knives for telling the story of Jesus by people who did not understand.
Move your finger across to the other end of the table, the left side of the table with the picture facing away from you toward the children. Then circle the group of three disciples there.	At the other end of the table is the last group of three. They are Matthew, Jude and Simon the Zealot.

MOVEMENTS	WORDS
Point to Matthew. With the picture facing away from you toward the children, Matthew is standing to the left of Philip, four places to the left of Jesus.	Here is Matthew. He was a tax collector from Capernaum until Jesus called him. Matthew followed Jesus and later wrote down his story of Jesus, "The Gospel of Matthew." It is the first book in the New Testament.
Move the shield for Matthew down from the row of shields along the top of the picture so that it rests right over his head.	Here is Matthew's symbol. It has three money bags on it to help us remember that he was a hated tax collector before Jesus called him and Matthew found peace.
Point to Jude. With the picture facing away from you toward the children, Jude is standing to the left of Matthew, five places to the left of Jesus.	This is Jude. His name almost sounds like "Judas." The next-to-last book in the New Testament may be a letter by Jude.
Move the shield for Jude down from the row of shields along the top of the picture so that it rests right over his head.	His symbol is a ship sailing, because he went across the sea to tell the story of Jesus.
Point to Simon. With the picture facing away from you toward the children, Simon is standing at the farthest left of the table.	Here is Simon. He was a fighter for his people and for God's law, so he was called "the Zealot." He was also a fisherman.
Move the shield for Simon down from the row of shields along the top of the picture so that it rests right over his head.	The symbol of Simon is a fish and a book. The fish helps us remember that he was a fisherman who became someone who fished for people to show them the truth about life. The book is the book of that truth. It stands for the Bible and especially the story of Jesus written down there.
Sit back and pause a little longer than after each apostle's presentation.	
Sweep your hand across all the apostles and then return to touch the shield above each head.	These are the Twelve, the apostles, and these are their symbols.

Now, I wonder which one of the Twelve you like best?

I wonder which one was the most important?

I wonder which one is most like you? Where are you in this story? |

MOVEMENTS

When the wondering subsides, put the material away and begin to help the children decide what work they are going to get out.

WORDS

I wonder if we can leave any of the Twelve out and still have all of this story that we need?

LESSON 10

THE GOOD SHEPHERD AND WORLD COMMUNION

LESSON NOTES

FOCUS: THE GOOD SHEPHERD AND HOLY COMMUNION

- LITURGICAL ACTION
- CORE PRESENTATION

THE MATERIAL

- LOCATION: FOCAL SHELVES
- PIECES: GOOD SHEPHERD, SHEEP, SHEEPFOLD, TABLE, PRIEST, PEOPLE OF THE WORLD, SMALL CONTAINER HOLDING A PATEN AND CHALICE
- UNDERLAY: 2 CIRCLES COVERED IN GREEN FELT

BACKGROUND

The images of the Good Shepherd and Holy Communion deepen each other's interpretation when set side by side like this. One does not need to step outside the domain of religious language into the language of philosophy or science, for example, to talk *about* the two religious images or interpret them. One can remain *within* religious language, meditating, while the images disclose the depths in each other.

For older children, you can also place other presentations side by side. For example, lay out the story of the Exodus (pp. 65-72, *The Complete Guide to Godly Play, Volume 2*) next to this story. Ask, "I wonder what in *this* story (the Exodus) belongs in *this* story (the Good Shepherd and World Communion)?" and *vice versa*.

Note: This lesson was suggested by the work of Sofia Cavalletti. The reader should be aware, however, that both the teaching material and the lesson are substantially changed and put to a different use in Godly Play than in her work. Please see *The Complete Guide to Godly Play, Volume 1*, Chapter 6, pp. 86-107, "Entering the Tradition," for further information.

NOTES ON THE MATERIAL

In an ideal setup, the focal shelves are the shelf unit directly opposite the door that the children enter. The Holy Family sits in the center of the top shelf. To the right of the Holy Family as you face the shelves is one green circle with the figure of the Good Shepherd, the sheepfold and his sheep. (The sheepfold is a set of hinged wooden fence pieces.) On the shelf below the Good Shepherd and his sheep, there is another green circle with a table standing at its center. On the shelf below the second circle, there is a basket that holds a priest, the people of the world and a small container. The container holds a paten and chalice to represent the bread and wine.

SPECIAL NOTES

As you can see, this is a core presentation for the liturgical action part of the Christian tradition of communion, as conceived of in Godly Play. It is not included among the parable lessons, because parables function in a different way than liturgical action, although there is always some overlap. This presentation does tell a story, but it is not part of the sacred story materials because it focuses on the liturgical action and the symbols by which that action carries its meaning to us and to which we respond.

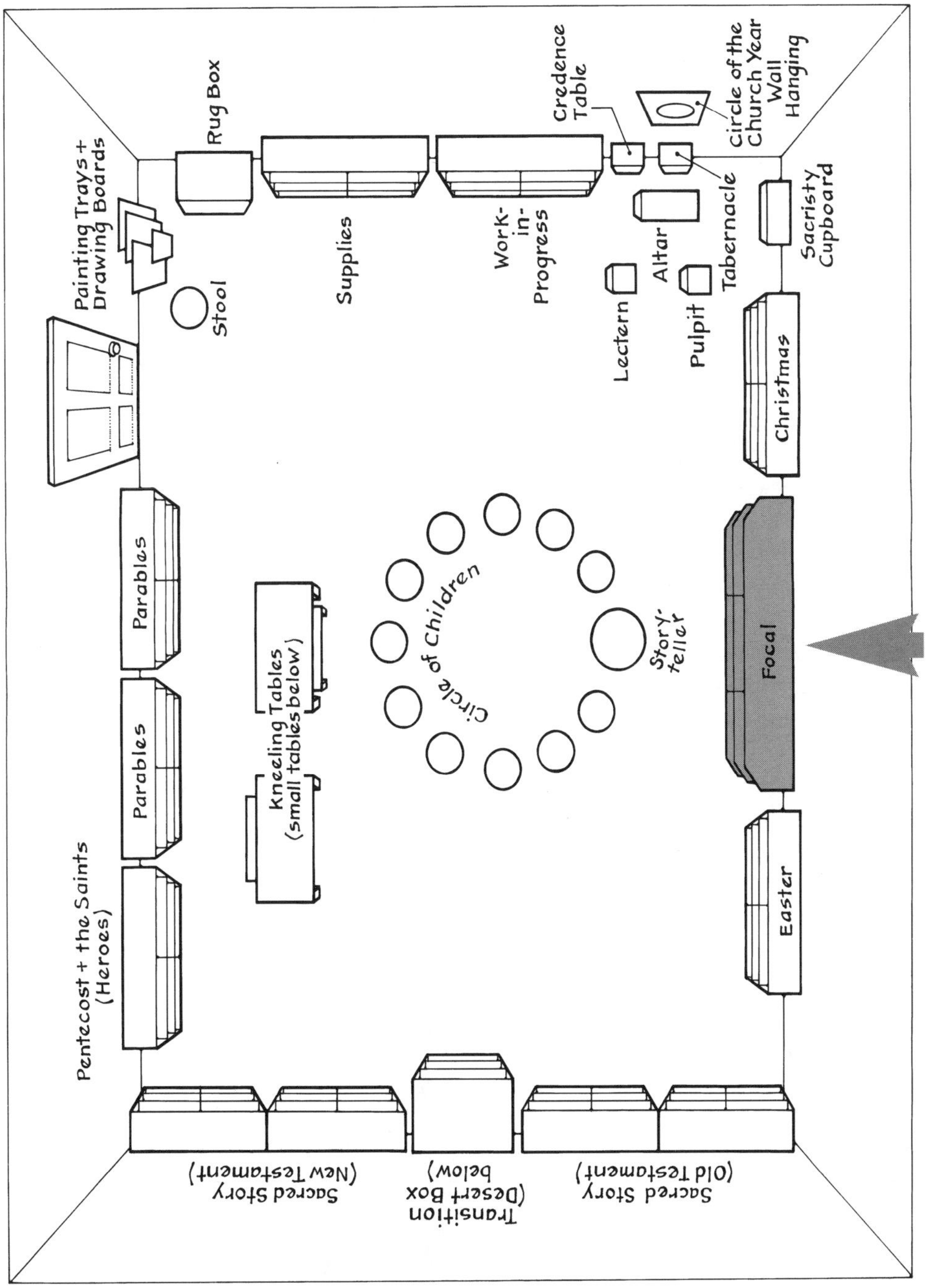
Rug Box
Painting Trays + Drawing Boards
Stool
Supplies
Work-in-Progress
Credence Table
Circle of the Church Year Wall Hanging
Tabernacle
Altar
Lectern
Pulpit
Sacristy Cupboard
Christmas
Focal
Easter
Story-teller
Circle of Children
Kneeling Tables (small tables below)
Parables
Parables
Pentecost + the Saints (Heroes)
Sacred Story (New Testament)
Transition (Desert Box below)
Sacred Story (Old Testament)

WHERE TO FIND MATERIALS

MOVEMENTS

Even though the material is right behind you, on the focal shelves, get up and walk around the circle to find the material. This is much more dramatic than merely reaching out to pull the pieces off the shelves. The children will gain a better sense of where the material is.

Carry the material carefully, with two hands, as you want the children to carry it. First bring the green circle with the Good Shepherd, the sheepfold and the sheep to the storytelling circle. Place it in front of where you will be sitting. Then return to the shelf for the second circle with the table on it.

Bring the second green circle to the storytelling circle. Then return to the shelves and bring the basket with the people of the world and the small container.

Put the two green circles next to each other, touching. The one on the right in front of you, the storyteller, is the Good Shepherd, and the one on your left is the Table. Put the basket to the right and a little behind where you are sitting. The point is to get this out of the way, so it will not distract the children until you are ready to use it.

The sheepfold, sheep and shepherd are arranged as shown here.

WORDS

➤ Watch carefully where I go so you will know where to find this material. Watch with your eyes.

➤ You see, there is a lot to bring. This is big work. Watch carefully.

THE SHEPHERD AND THE SHEEPFOLD (STORYTELLER'S PERSPECTIVE)

MOVEMENTS

WORDS

Sit for a brief time to let the children settle. If they have trouble getting ready, work with them until they are settled. Then begin.

➭ There was once someone who did such wonderful things and said such amazing things that people wondered who he was. Finally they just couldn't help it. They had to ask him who he was.

Touch the head of the Good Shepherd figure.

➭ When they asked him who he was, he said, "I am the Good Shepherd."

Run your thumb down the back of the neck of each sheep.

➭ "I know each one of the sheep by name, and they know the sound of my voice."

Move the Good Shepherd out of the sheepfold and around to your right. Move him halfway around to a position at the bottom of the circle in front of you. Then go back and move each one of the sheep to catch up with him. They stay in single file. Keep silence while you are doing this and just enjoy watching the sheep.

➭ "When I take the sheep from the sheepfold, they follow me."

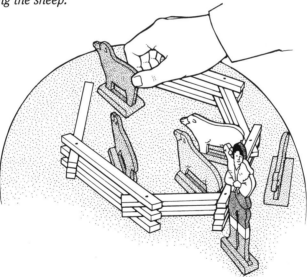

OUTSIDE THE SHEEPFOLD (STORYTELLER'S PERSPECTIVE)

Move the Good Shepherd from the bottom position on the right circle to the top position on the left circle. Take your time.

➭ "I walk in front of the sheep to show them the way."

MOVEMENTS	WORDS

APPROACHING THE TABLE (STORYTELLER'S PERSPECTIVE)

Move the sheep up to where the Good Shepherd is. Move them one at a time. Think about what is happening as you move them from one circle to the other.

➠ "I show them the way to the good grass."

Without saying anything else, move the Good Shepherd to the bottom position of the left-hand circle and move the sheep so that they are spread out equally now around the table but still turned as if they are following around the edge of the circle.

When all of the sheep are in position, move the Good Shepherd forward to stand behind the table (from the child's perspective). Turn all of the sheep so they are facing the table.

MOVEMENTS   WORDS

AROUND THE TABLE (STORYTELLER'S PERSPECTIVE)

MOVEMENTS	WORDS
Trace the outside rim of the table.	This is the table of the Good Shepherd.
Get the chalice and paten from the basket and place them on the table.	Here is the bread and wine of the Good Shepherd. Sometimes it seems like we need to have a little statue or something on the table to remind us that this is the table of the Good Shepherd, but the Good Shepherd is in the bread and the wine, so we don't really need anything to remind us.
Remove the Good Shepherd. Bring out the priest and move the priest into the position behind the table where the Good Shepherd was.	Sometimes someone comes to read the very words of the Good Shepherd, and to give us the bread and the wine.
Take one of the adult human figures from the basket. Show it to the children, then put it between the sheep. Continue doing this until all the adults from around the world are in place.	Sometimes the people of the world come to this table, and...
Take out the child figures and put them by the adult figures. Do not group the figures by gender, ethnicity or culture. The world no longer works like that.	...even the children come.

MOVEMENTS   **WORDS**

THE PEOPLE AROUND THE TABLE (STORYTELLER'S PERSPECTIVE)

Sit and look at the people of the world around the table for a moment, then begin the wondering.	Now I wonder if you have ever come close to this table?
	I wonder where this table could really be?
Trace the outline of the table with your finger. Don't hurry the children. Give them time to wonder.	I wonder if the people are happy around this table?
	I wonder if you have ever heard the words of the Good Shepherd?
	I wonder if you have ever come close to the bread and the wine?
	I wonder where the bread and the wine could really be?
Move your hand over both circles.	I wonder where this whole place could really be?
When the wondering draws to a close, turn the children's attention toward getting out their own work.	

LESSON 11

THE SYNAGOGUE AND THE UPPER ROOM

LESSON NOTES

FOCUS: THE HOLY WORD AND THE HOLY TABLE

- **LITURGICAL ACTION**
- **CORE PRESENTATION**

THE MATERIAL

- **LOCATION: EASTER SHELVES**
- **PIECES: MODEL OF A SYNAGOGUE, SCROLL, BASKET, LECTERN, FIGURE OF JESUS, MODEL OF THE UPPER ROOM, TABLE**
- **UNDERLAY: NONE**

BACKGROUND

The first part of the presentation evokes the Liturgy of the Word, which the Christian Church developed from the readings of the Jewish synagogue. The second part of the presentation evokes the liturgy of the table, which Jesus instituted during the Last Supper in the upper room. The synagogue and upper room are joined together to form a model of Christian worship, the joining of the Old and New Testaments, and much more.

The event in the synagogue is based mainly on Luke 4:16-30, but there are overtones of Mark 6:1-6 and Matthew 13:53-58. Luke tells the larger story, but Matthew and Mark have the famous saying about a prophet being without honor in his own country and in his own house.

Note: This lesson was suggested by the work of Sofia Cavalletti. The reader should be aware, however, that both the teaching material and the lesson are substantially changed and put to a different use in Godly Play than in her work. Please see *The Complete Guide to Godly Play, Volume 1*, Chapter 6, pp. 86-107, "Entering the Tradition," for further information.

NOTES ON THE MATERIAL

Find this material on the far right of the top shelf of the Easter shelves, to the right of the material for the Faces of Easter. The material has two main parts, a model of a synagogue and a model of the upper room.

The synagogue model includes a basket with a scroll in it and a lectern from which the scroll is read. On the scroll is written Isaiah 4:18-19. The back wall of the synagogue is made up of three pieces that can be removed. The outer piece of the back wall has a menorah on one side and a cross on the other. The two inner pieces of the back wall will form two walls of the finished building made by joining the synagogue to the upper room.

The model of the upper room has a table in it. There is also a cast metal figure of Jesus, used in both the synagogue and the upper room. On the shelf, this figure can be left standing in the upper room. There are no figures for the synagogue congregation or for the Twelve, because in this presentation the focus is entirely on Jesus.

SPECIAL NOTES

Storytelling Tip: When telling this story, be careful with your movements, especially when lifting the two back pieces from the synagogue wall. It's easy to knock them down with a loud clatter and disrupt the mood of the lesson.

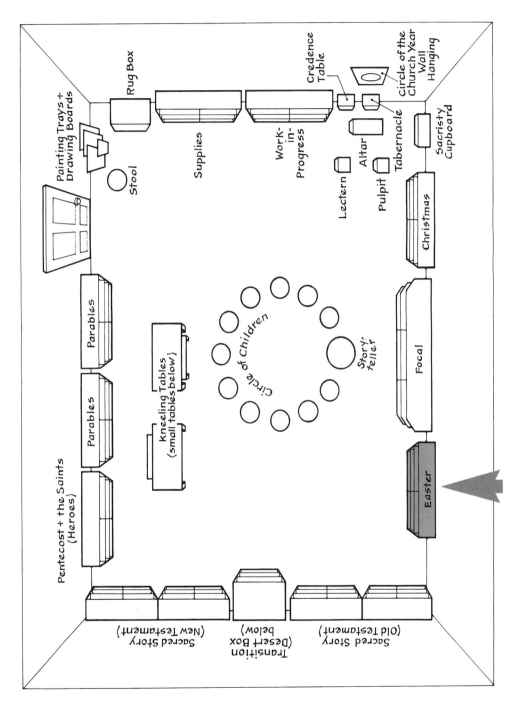

WHERE TO FIND MATERIALS

MOVEMENTS

When the children are settled in the circle, get the model of the synagogue, the model of the upper room and the figure of Jesus. Move the synagogue into the circle of children. The cross on the back wall is hidden, facing you. The menorah on the back wall is toward the children.

Place the Jesus figure in the model synagogue.

WORDS

➠ This is the synagogue in the village of Nazareth, where Jesus grew up.

After Jesus came back from the desert across the river Jordan, he came home to Nazareth.

➠ Jesus went to the synagogue as was his custom. He went to the reading place and unrolled the scroll of Isaiah.

THE SYNOGOGUE (CHILDREN'S PERSPECTIVE)

Unroll the scroll that is in the basket and read from it. This is Luke 4:18-19.

➠ This is what he read:

"The Spirit of the Lord is upon me, because he has anointed me to preach good news to the poor. He has sent me to proclaim release to the captives and recovery of sight to the blind, to let the oppressed go free, to proclaim the year of the Lord's favor."

Jesus rolled up the scroll and sat down. When they began to discuss the reading, he said something like, "Today this scripture has been fulfilled in your hearing. It has come true."

MOVEMENTS	WORDS
	The people heard what Jesus said and became angry. He is not the Messiah! They knew who he was. He was Mary and Joseph's son.
Move the Jesus figure out from the synagogue to stand in front of it.	They took Jesus to the edge of the village where there was a cliff. They wanted to throw him off...
Remove the Jesus figure and place it beside you.	...but he walked back through the crowd and into the hills.
	Many days went by. He gathered the Twelve. He did his work. Then he turned to Jerusalem for the last time. Jesus and the Twelve came into the city on a Sunday. He taught in the Temple on Monday, Tuesday and Wednesday. On Thursday, the temple guards could not find him.
Move the upper room model into the middle of the circle of children and place it beside the synagogue model. Put the Jesus figure behind the table in the middle.	That evening Jesus and the Twelve went through the dark and narrow streets. They climbed upstairs in a house. They went into the upper room and shared their last supper together.

THE UPPER ROOM (CHILDREN'S PERSPECTIVE)

After they had eaten everything they wanted to eat, Jesus did something very strange. He took a piece of bread, gave thanks to God for it, broke it and shared it with the Twelve.

Then he said something like, "When you share the bread like this, I will be there."

But he was there!

MOVEMENTS

Move the synagogue model around in front of the upper room, with its back wall touching the front edge of the upper room. Take the outer piece of the back wall of the synagogue off. Turn it around, so the cross faces the children. Slide it onto the center back wall of the upper room.

Take the two remaining panels that make up the inner back wall of the synagogue and slide one into each of the slots formed by the inner front edges of the upper room and the outer back edges of the synagogue. This makes two models into one model of a cross-shaped church.

WORDS

Then he took a cup of wine, gave thanks to God for it and shared it with them.

Then he said something like, "When you share the wine like this, I will be there."

He was always saying things like that. What could he mean? They did not understand at first, but they did not forget. Later they would understand.

Now watch carefully.

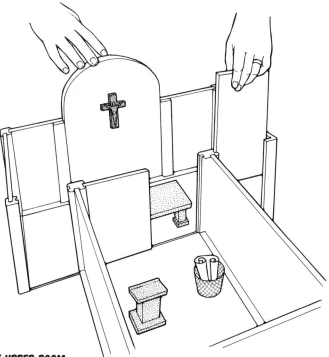

CHANGING THE SYNAGOGUE AND THE UPPER ROOM INTO THE CHURCH (CHILDREN'S PERSPECTIVE)

MOVEMENTS

Trace the structure with your finger.

Point to the reading lectern. Point to the table. Trace the areas of the synagogue and the upper room and then trace the whole structure again. Do not say anything. Let the children make the discoveries.

If they do not say anything aloud, continue to wonder silently and then begin to put the material away.

Return to the circle, then turn the children's attention toward getting out their own work.

WORDS

 Look. I wonder what this could be?

➧ Hmm.

➧ Now watch carefully where I go to put this away, so you will always know where to find it.

CIRCLE OF THE HOLY EUCHARIST

LESSON NOTES

FOCUS: WHAT HAPPENS IN CHURCH EACH SUNDAY

- LITURGICAL ACTION
- CORE PRESENTATION

THE MATERIAL

- LOCATION: EASTER SHELVES
- PIECES: TRAY-SHAPED BASKET, 1 CARD PICTURING JESUS IN THE UPPER ROOM, 1 CARD PICTURING A READER IN THE SYNAGOGUE, SET OF 17 CARDS SHOWING THE MAJOR PARTS AND ACTS OF THE HOLY EUCHARIST
- UNDERLAY: GREEN CIRCLE

BACKGROUND

This presentation and material, another in the series of lessons developing themes in the Holy Eucharist, helps children pull together the sequence of liturgical actions and images from the Godly Play presentations they have seen and from their church's Sunday celebration. Adjust it, as necessary, to fit what happens in your church.

We lay out the lesson on a green circle, echoing the green used in the presentation of the Good Shepherd and World Communion. Its circular shape is important, because when the Holy Eucharist concludes, it is ready to begin again, waiting for us to take part. The gift of its way to make meaning is always there, inviting us to begin again.

The pieces laid out on the green circle are flat, two-dimensional pieces rather than the three-dimensional pieces the children have seen so far in this series. This lesson helps children take a step toward abstraction and the integration of the parts into the wholeness of the Eucharist.

NOTES ON THE MATERIAL

Find this material on the far left of the middle shelf of the Easter shelves, directly underneath the material for the Mystery of Easter. The material is a tray-shaped basket holding a green felt underlay and a set of wooden or foamcore cards.

As the lesson begins, the presentation retells the story of the Synagogue and the Upper Room, but this time, instead of using three-dimensional material, you put an orange card in the center of the green circle showing a line drawing of someone reading in the synagogue and then above it a yellow-gold card with a line drawing of Jesus and the Twelve in the upper room. These two cards measure 4" x 6-1/2".

You then lay out cards around the edge of the circle to show the major acts in the sequence of the Holy Eucharist. If necessary, make adjustments to the cards we suggest to match the practice of your congregation. Change any words of the story, too, to match what is actually said and done in your church.

The key card bears the title "The Holy Eucharist." This is an orange card that measures 5" x 7-1/2". The center of the card shows the picture of a golden cross. Two additional cards, each measuring 4" x 6-1/2", mark the two major divisions of the Holy Eucharist: "The Word of God" and "The Holy Communion." The Word of God card is orange with a drawing of an open Bible. The Holy Communion card is yellow-gold with a drawing of a host and chalice to represent the bread and wine.

We suggest eight orange cards, each 4" x 6-1/2", with the following labels for the Liturgy of the Word:
• Opening and the Collect of the Day
• The Lessons: The Old Testament—The Letters
• Lesson: the Gospel
• The Sermon
• The Nicene Creed
• The Prayers of the People
• Confession of Sin
• The Peace

We suggest six yellow-gold cards, each 4" x 6-1/2", with the following labels for the Liturgy of Holy Communion:
• Offertory
• The Great Thanksgiving
• Prayer of Consecration
• The Breaking of the Bread
• Communion
• Blessing and Dismissal

SPECIAL NOTES

Using in Church: Please note that extra sets of these cards make a wonderful way for children to follow and name what is going on in the liturgy of your church. For use during church, mount them on cardboard and laminate them. Punch holes In the cards and put a ring through them to fix the sequence for the children. They can then follow the action by flipping the cards.

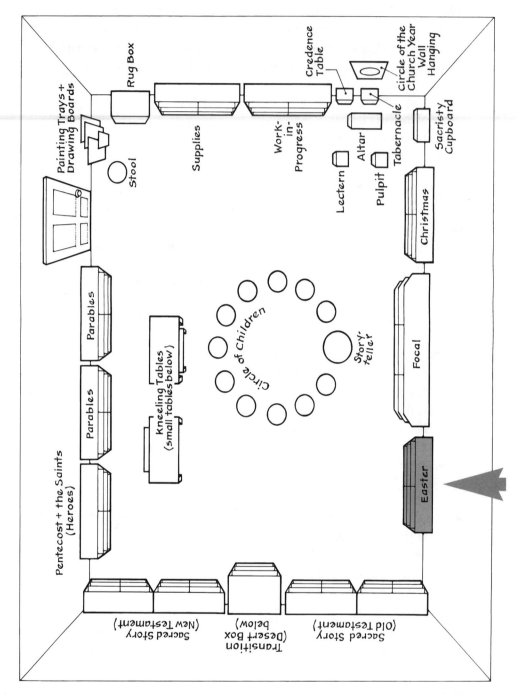

WHERE TO FIND MATERIALS

MOVEMENTS

When the children are settled in the circle, go to the Easter shelves and bring the basket with its underlay and cards to the circle.

Take out the underlay as if it were the underlay for a parable. Leave it crumpled in the middle of the circle for a moment, and then smooth it out. It is the same color as the underlay for the parable of the Good Shepherd, but it is round, not irregular, in shape.

The children may or may not respond, helping to build a metaphor and connecting it to previous lessons. If they do respond, wonder with them for a few moments, but this does not need to go on as long as with a parable.

Then begin the story.

Place the card for the synagogue in the center of the underlay, facing the children.

WORDS

Watch where I go, so you will always know where to find this lesson.

I wonder what this could be.

After Jesus was baptized and had come back over the Jordan River from the desert, he went home to his village of Nazareth.

He went into the synagogue and read from the scroll of Isaiah:

"The Spirit of the Lord is upon me, because he has anointed me to preach good news to the poor. He has sent me to proclaim release to the captives and recovery of sight to the blind, to let the oppressed go free, to proclaim the year of the Lord's favor" (Luke 4:18-19).

Jesus rolled up the scroll, handed it to an attendant and sat down. He then said to them, "Today this scripture has been fulfilled in your hearing."

The people of Jesus' village said something like, "This is not the Messiah, the Anointed One. He thinks he is God, but he is just Mary and Joseph's son."

They took Jesus to the edge of the village where there was a cliff. They wanted to throw him off, but he walked back through the crowd and into the hills.

MOVEMENTS	WORDS
Place the card with Jesus and the Twelve in the center of the underlay, above the synagogue card, facing the children.	Jesus then gathered the Twelve to help him. He did many wonderful things, but then he and the Twelve went to Jerusalem for the last time. On Thursday evening of that last week, Jesus and the Twelve met in an upper room. After they had everything they wanted to eat and drink, Jesus did something very strange. He took a piece of bread, and when he had given thanks, he broke it. Then he said something like, "Whenever you do this and share the bread, I will be there." They must have thought, "What do you mean? You *are* here." He then took a cup of wine. He gave thanks to God for it and then said something like, "Whenever you share the cup of wine like this, I will be there." The Twelve did not understand, but they never forgot. Later they would understand.
Place the Holy Eucharist card facing the children at the children's top of the circle (from the children's point of view), the point nearest you.	This was how the Holy Eucharist began. It has two parts.
Point to the orange card of the synagogue already placed at the center of the underlay.	First there is the Liturgy of the Word of God.
Place the card for "The Word of God" just to the left of the Holy Eucharist card as you face it.	The Word of God is when we read from the scriptures and hear the sermon.
Point to the yellow card of the upper room already placed at the center of the underlay.	
Place the card for "The Holy Communion" near the children's bottom of the circle, the point farthest from you. Place it a little to your right of the midpoint of the circle you will soon lay out.	The second part is the Holy Communion.

MOVEMENTS

You will now place cards in a clock-wise fashion between the card for "The Word of God" and the card for "The Holy Communion." First place the card for the "Opening and the Collect of the Day."

Place the card for "The Lessons: The Old Testament—The Letters."

Place the card for "The Lessons: The Gospel."

Place the card for "The Sermon."

Place the card for "The Nicene Creed."

Place the card for "The Prayers of the People."

Place the card for "The Confession of Sin."

WORDS

When the Holy Eucharist begins, there is sometimes music and a procession but there does not need to be. The priest says, "Blessed be God: Father, Son and Holy Spirit." Prayers are said to help us get ready. One of the prayers changes each week. It is called a "collect."

Someone then comes forward and reads from the Old Testament. Next we often read or sing a psalm. Then someone reads something from the New Testament, perhaps part of one of Paul's letters.

After that the most important reading happens. It is the Gospel. The Gospel Book is carried very carefully to the center, and sometimes there are even people on each side of the reader holding tall candles called torches.

After the reading of God's Word in the Bible, someone comes and tries to say something about what was read. It is not easy. Sometimes you have to listen very carefully. This is hard for the grownups, too.

After the sermon we all say together what we believe. One person got to say something in the sermon. Now we all speak. Together we say the Nicene Creed.

Next we pray for everyone. We pray for people who are sick or in trouble. We pray for those who are hungry or lost. We pray for peace. We also give thanks for all the wonderful things that happen in life, like babies being born, people getting married and sick people getting well. We give thanks for good governments and for the lives of people who have died.

The leader then says, "Let us confess our sins against God and our neighbor." No one is perfect.

Sometimes even when good people try hard, they still make mistakes. We need to say we are sorry to people we have hurt and to God. It is good to confess one's sins. It helps us do better next time.

After we confess our sins all together, the priest tells us that God forgive us. Jesus forgives us, too. He shows us *how* to be good, and he also makes us *strong* to be good. The Holy Spirit gives us the power to find and live the right way.

MOVEMENTS

Place the card for "The Peace" at the children's bottom of the circle. This brings the cards for the Word of God to an end.

Now you have come to the card for "The Holy Communion." The next set of cards will also be placed in clockwise fashion, from the card for "The Holy Communion" to the card for "The Holy Eucharist."

Place the card for the "Offertory."

Place the card for "The Great Thanksgiving."

Place the card for the "Prayer of Consecration."

Place the card for "The Breaking of Bread."

Place the card for "Communion."

WORDS

After we are forgiven, we can't help but want to be close to everyone. People turn to each other and say, "The peace of the Lord be always with you." People say back, "And also with you."

Look, now we change. The time of the readings and thinking about them is over. The prayers have been said. We now get ready to do something very different. We prepare for Holy Communion. It helps us go where words and thinking alone cannot take us.

People bring gifts of money and other things to the altar. Above all they bring the gifts of bread and wine.

The gifts are received. When everything is ready the priest begins the Great Thanksgiving: "The Lord be with you." This is a time to lift up our hearts, to give thanks and praise. What is beginning to happen is a great mystery.

We remember the Last Supper of Jesus and the Twelve and then gradually we are there and it is here.

The priest prays for the Holy Spirit to sanctify the bread and wine, to change them from their ordinary use to this special use. The priest also prays for us to be sanctified, so we will be able to faithfully receive this holy Sacrament and serve God in unity, constancy and peace, and at the last day to join with all the saints in the joy of God's eternal kingdom.

We then say together the Lord's Prayer and hear especially the part: "Give us this day our daily bread."

The celebrant holds the bread up so we can see it, and breaks it. Sometimes you can even hear it crack. We give thanks for Jesus being with us and the celebrant reminds us that the bread and wine are for us, gifts from God.

People come forward now to receive the holy bread and holy wine. Jesus is with us in the bread and wine and we are all together, all over the world, and with all who have lived and died in this huge family of families called the Church.

MOVEMENTS

Place the card for the "Blessing and Dismissal."

The green underlay now has cards all around its circumference. Sit back and enjoy the completed presentation for a moment or two.

WORDS

Everything is put away and we get ready to go out. The leader says something like, "Let us go forth in the name of Christ." And we always say, all together, "Thanks be to God!"

The Holy Eucharist is now ready to begin again

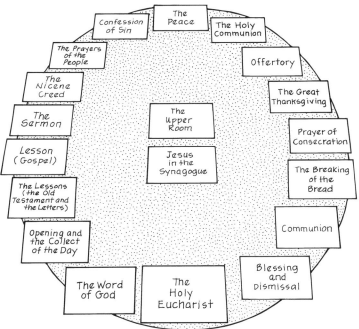

THE COMPLETED CIRCLE (STORYTELLER'S PERSPECTIVE)

Move your hand around the circumference.

Now I wonder what part of the Holy Eucharist you like best?

I wonder what part is the most important part?

I wonder what part is especially for you?

I wonder if we could leave anything out and still have everything we need?

MOVEMENTS

When the wondering is finished, carefully replace the cards in the basket. As you replace the cards, name them once again. Don't hurry. Fold up the underlay and place it in the basket. Carry the basket with two hands and place it on the shelf.

Return to the circle.

WORDS

➤ Here is the Holy Eucharist. Here is the part called the Word of God. Etc.

➤ Now what work would you like to get out today?

ENRICHMENT LESSON

SYMBOLS OF THE HOLY EUCHARIST

LESSON NOTES

FOCUS: SPECIAL MATERIALS FOR THE HOLY EUCHARIST

- LITURGICAL ACTION
- ENRICHMENT PRESENTATION

THE MATERIAL

- LOCATION: AREA OF THE ROOM SET APART FOR THESE SYMBOLS
- PIECES: WOODEN LITURGICAL FURNISHINGS (TABERNACLE, CREDENCE TABLE, LECTERN, ALTAR, PULPIT, SACRISTY CUPBOARD); CLOTH FURNISHINGS (SEASONAL HANGINGS, FAIR LINEN, PURIFICATORS); OTHER FURNISHINGS (BIBLE, CANDLES, CANDLE STICKS, CANDLE SNUFFER, ALTAR BOOK, GOSPEL BOOK, CRUETS FOR WATER AND WINE, CIBORIUM, CHALICE, PATEN); BOX OF PROMPTING CARDS
- UNDERLAY: NONE

BACKGROUND

This presentation requires an elaborate set of materials described below. The reading portions of the presentation are intended for children from about the second grade on.

Before the presentation, ask your sacristan or a member of the church's altar guild to give a tour of the sacristy, where they keep the things used for Holy Communion. Ask those who care for these symbols to show them to the children, where they belong, and how they are used.

This lesson supports children by introducing and naming the actual symbols, so they can work independently with the classroom material. In the classroom, they can use all their senses instead of primarily relying on sight. This gives them more experience to draw on when they see actual symbols, such as the chalice and paten, etc., in church.

The fundamental goal of this lesson is to convey that these things are set apart from ordinary use for special use in the Holy Eucharist. To show this, we give almost everything another name. For example, a cup is no longer a cup. It becomes a chalice. This new language sharpens all the children's senses to participate in the liturgical action when the congregation gathers, both in the church and elsewhere.

NOTES ON THE MATERIAL

This material is kept in an area of the room all its own. Instead of bringing the material to a group of children, you bring a small group (not more than three children) to the materials and work with them there.

The setup includes:
- a small wooden tabernacle (box), attached to the wall
- a credence table, attached to the wall
- a sacristy cupboard
- an altar
- a pulpit
- a lectern

The diagram on page 117 shows the layout of the above items.

There is also a box that holds "prompting cards" for naming the symbols of the Holy Eucharist. The wooden materials and cards are made commercially by Godly Play Resources. They do not sell the remaining materials for this presentation.

Other materials to include are child-sized communion materials, such as could be found in a portable communion kit. (Contact a church supplies distributor that ministers to your denomination.) You'll also want the liturgical materials for your denomination, such as *The Book of Common Prayer* (Episcopalian), *The Lutheran Book of Worship*, etc.

SPECIAL NOTES

Classroom Management: The storyteller gathers not more than about three children who sit outside the setup in front of the altar. The storyteller sits inside, between the tabernacle and the altar. A child working alone sits where the storyteller does. When children are working in a group alone, they take turns being the one child who sits where the storyteller does. The other children sit facing the altar.

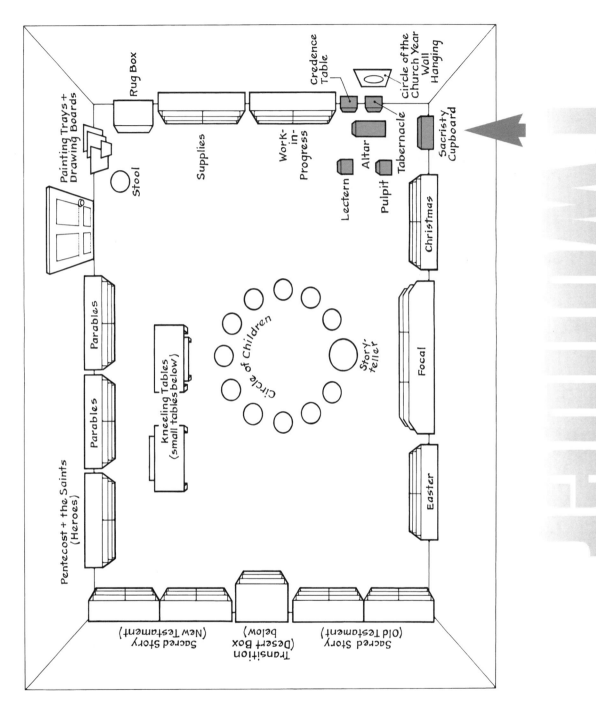

WHERE TO FIND MATERIALS

MOVEMENTS

WORDS

Bring the children with whom you are working to the area where the symbols are kept. Sit between the tabernacle and the altar. The children sit outside the setup, facing the altar.

For any symbol or symbols you choose to introduce in this presentation, use a three-step procedure in which you identify, name and value the symbol. For example, for the chalice, you would follow these three steps:

1. Point to the chalice.

➧ This is the chalice.

2. Let the children point out the chalice.

➧ Show me the chalice.

3. Point to the chalice.

➧ What is this?

With older children, you can elaborate this third step.

➧ Where is it kept? What is it used for?

When you have introduced several symbols, you can begin the wondering.

➧ I wonder which symbol you like best?

I wonder which symbol is the most important?

I wonder *where* you see these symbols in church?

I wonder *when* you see these symbols in church?

I wonder what the leader does with these symbols?

I wonder what these symbols say?

I wonder how you come close to these symbols?

With children who read, you can show them how to label each symbol by placing a card with its name on it beside or on the symbol. Children can also completely prepare the area with everything needed for the Holy Eucharist.

MOVEMENTS

WORDS

Finally you or the children can read the Eucharist from your church's liturgy and use each of the symbols at the appropriate time and in an appropriate way. The storyteller needs to support this the first time a child or group of children participates. Sit nearby and prompt when necessary.

LESSON 13
THE MYSTERY OF PENTECOST

LESSON NOTES

FOCUS: THE PEOPLE OF GOD MEET GOD IN A NEW WAY

● LITURGICAL ACTION

● CORE PRESENTATION

THE MATERIAL

● LOCATION: SACRED STORY (NEW TESTAMENT) SHELVES

● PIECES: RED PARABLE-SIZED BOX, 12 BROWN FELT STRIPS, 6 PLAIN WOODEN
  BLOCKS, SYMBOLS OF THE TWELVE

● UNDERLAY: RED

BACKGROUND

Something strange happened on Pentecost that had to do with "tongues" of fire and
speaking so that no matter what "tongues" others spoke, they could understand what
was meant. Did their tongues burn in their mouths as they began to communicate in
a new way? Was the communication nonverbal? Can God's presence be communi-
cated in words?

The strange event on the Day of Pentecost reminds us of the earlier day when communication was fractured so that what before had been understandable was now
babel, a confusion of tongues. That is why this lesson begins with the Tower of Babel,
from Genesis 11:1-9. This presentation also draws on stories found in Mark 16:19-
20, Luke 24:50-53 and Acts 1:5-14; 2:1-12.

In future volumes, we will describe materials for a whole set of Pentecost liturgical
shelves. For now, we need to include the red box of the Mystery of Pentecost to complete the cycle of three great times in the Circle of the Church Year. We have lessons
for the Mystery of Christmas (*The Complete Guide to Godly Play, Volume 3,* pp. 56-
63), for the Mystery of Easter (this volume, pp. 27-31) and, now, for the Mystery of
Pentecost.

NOTES ON THE MATERIAL

Until materials for the Pentecost liturgical shelves are published, place this material on the right side of the top shelf of the New Testament section of the Sacred Story shelves, as you stand facing the shelves. Only the materials for "Paul's Discovery" and "The Part that Hasn't Been Written Yet" will be farther to the right.

The box is red and the same size and shape as the parable boxes. Inside the box is a red felt underlay that matches the size and shape of the underlay used in the Parable of the Good Shepherd (*The Complete Guide to Godly Play, Volume 3,* pp. 77-86). There are also twelve brown felt strips (about 1" x 10") that match the strips from the Parable of the Good Shepherd. The box also holds six plain wooden blocks (about 3" x 3") that can be stacked to make a Tower of Babel. Finally, there is a container that holds the symbols of the Twelve.

SPECIAL NOTES

Storytelling Tip: This lesson resembles a parable. Like a parable, it's meant to be symbolic, rather than historical. Stacking the blocks, however, creates a three-dimensional structure, adding concreteness to the story. We balance this concreteness by using symbols instead of figures for the apostles and brown strips instead of a model for Jerusalem. This moves the presentation toward the parabolic rather than the concrete.

Our intent is to leave room for God to enter and play. Making the presentation too realistic blocks the mystery, shuts the door to God's presence, and turns the event into past history instead of present encounter.

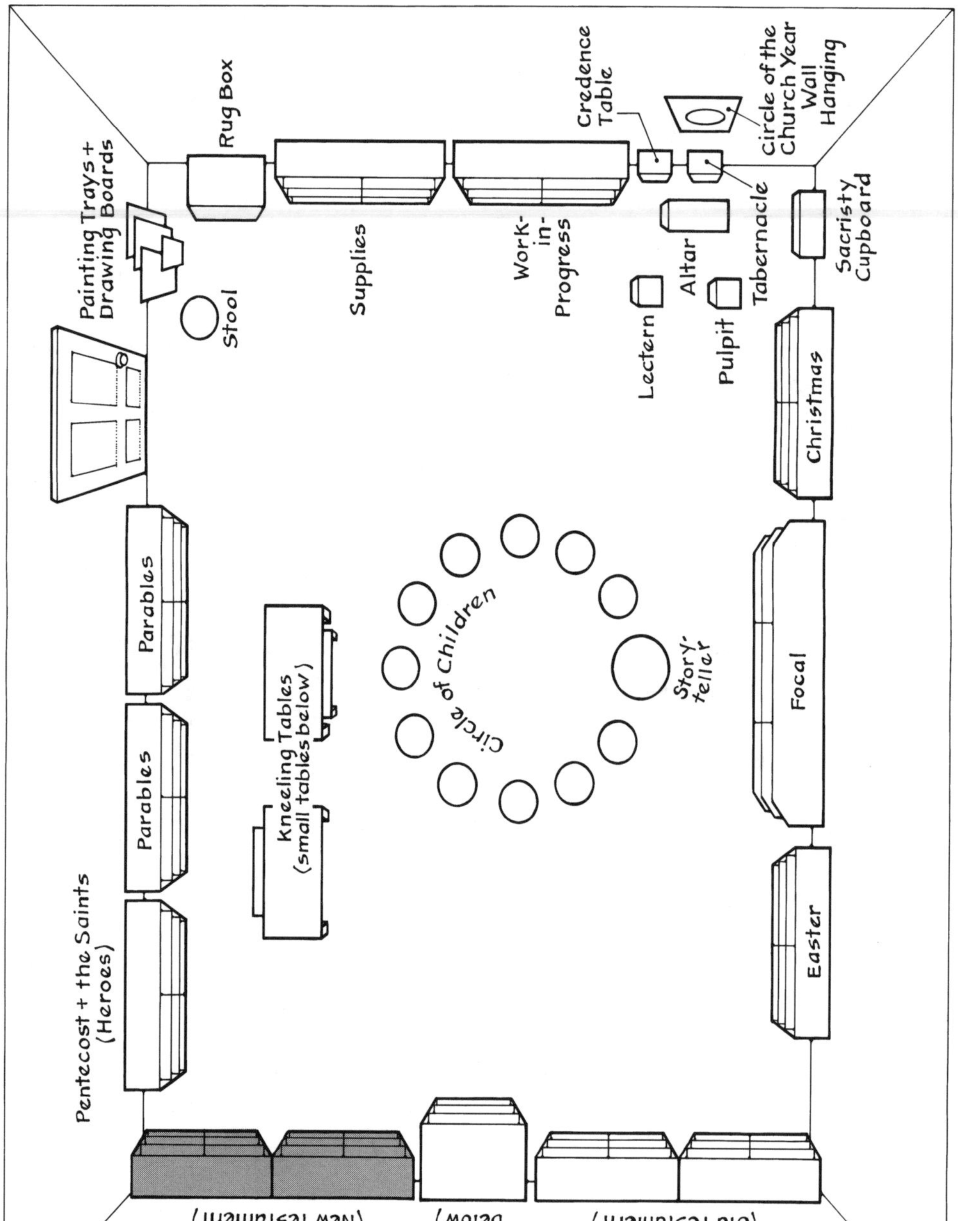
Rug Box
Painting Trays + Drawing Boards
Stool
Supplies
Work-in-Progress
Credence Table
Circle of the Church Year Wall Hanging
Tabernacle
Sacristy Cupboard
Altar
Lectern
Pulpit
Christmas
Focal
Easter
Story-teller
Circle of Children
Kneeling Tables (small tables below)
Parables
Parables
Pentecost + the Saints (Heroes)
Sacred Story (New Testament)
Transition (Desert Box below)
Sacred Story (Old Testament)

WHERE TO FIND MATERIALS

MOVEMENTS

When the children are settled, go to the shelves where the material is located.

Pick up the red box with mystery and amazement.

Bring the box to the circle and place it in the center of the children. Sit back. Relax. Be present.

Move the box to your side with the lid propped up on the side facing the children, so they won't be tempted to peek at what is coming out of the box next.

Take out the underlay. Leave it crumpled in the middle of the circle for a moment and then smooth it out.

Pause and begin.

Place the first block down in the middle of the underlay.

Put the second block down on top of the first.

Slowly build up the blocks as you tell the story.

Keep building block by block, in such a way that the tower becomes more precarious.

The blocks now need to fall of their own weight.

WORDS

Watch carefully where I go so you will always know where to find this material.

This is the Mystery of Pentecost.

I wonder what could be inside? This looks like a parable box, but it is red. It must be like a parable and yet not be a parable. I have an idea. Let's look inside and see what is there.

There are some things inside to tell the story, but there is nothing else to put down to help us get ready. I guess all we can do, then, is begin.

There was once a great tower.

Everyone working on the tower spoke the same language and worked together.

But as the tower grew taller and taller, they began to talk in different ways.

The tower came close to God, but the people forgot why they were building it. They grew so proud of themselves that they began to think they were greater builders than God. Each group thought it was better than any of the others.

A huge noise replaced their talking. It made no sense. Everyone was babbling.

Soon the tower fell down, so it was called the Tower of Babel. The language of the people of the earth was shattered and broke into splinters. Each one was beautiful, but it was broken.

MOVEMENTS

Slowly pick up the blocks and put them back into the box. Sit back and pause. Reflect silently on what has happened.

Lay out the brown felt strips in a rectangle, leaving an open space for a doorway.

Place all the symbols of the Twelve, except the symbol for Matthias (the symbol with a sword and book), inside the rectangle. There is no symbol for Judas.

Move the symbols for the disciples outside Jerusalem and place them in a circle.

With your palms turned up, raise your hands upward together.

Turn your hands over and hold them over the circle of disciples and then allow one hand to move slowly down and lightly touch the disciples.

Add the symbol of Matthias to the group, which is now inside "Jerusalem." Crowd them together in the center of the rectangle made from the brown strips.

WORDS

Thousands of years passed. Then Jesus died on the cross, but somehow he was still with the people around him as he is with us. They kept seeing him, and they couldn't let him go. Then one day something amazing happened.

The disciples were in Jerusalem.

Here they are: Peter, James, John, Andrew, Philip, Bartholomew, Matthew, Thomas, James the Less, Simon and Jude. There are only eleven disciples because Judas had already killed himself.

Jesus took them outside of Jerusalem to a Mountain called Olivet, or as far as Bethany.

Jesus then went up, and soon the Holy Spirit would come down.

The eleven disciples went back into the city. They were full of joy and went to the Temple to pray. They then went to the upper room and, with God's help, decided that Matthias would take Judas' place.

On Sunday the Twelve were together again. Suddenly there was a sound like a mighty wind rushing in to be with them. It was the Holy Spirit. They became so full of its power that they seemed to be on fire. Their tongues burned in their mouths. They were so excited that people wondered what was going on.

When the disciples went out on the street, there were people there from many different countries. They spoke many different languages.

MOVEMENTS

WORDS

Everyone could see that the Twelve had come close to God—and God had come close to them—in a new way. It no longer mattered that they spoke different languages.

Place the symbols of the apostles radiating out from "Jerusalem."

The disciples had become apostles! They went out into all the world to tell this story.

Ever since, Pentecost has been celebrated to remember that day.

Sit back. Collect yourself. Breathe.

Now I wonder what part of this story you like best?

I wonder what the most important part could be?

I wonder where you are in the story? What part of the story is about you?

I wonder if we can leave out any part of this story and still have all the story we need?

I wonder if you have ever come close to something like this?

I wonder if there is anything in our church that reminds you of this?

When the wondering draws to a close, place everything back in the box. Take the box back to its shelf.

Now watch carefully where I go to put this lesson away. While I am putting it away, begin thinking about what you are going to get out for your work today.

Help the children choose their own work.

LESSON 14

PAUL'S DISCOVERY

LESSON NOTES

FOCUS: LIVING IN THE POWER OF THE HOLY SPIRIT

- ● SACRED STORY
- ● CORE PRESENTATION

THE MATERIAL

- ● LOCATION: SACRED STORY (NEW TESTAMENT) SHELVES
- ● PIECES: BOX CONTAINING 7 CARDS ILLUSTRATED WITH SCENES OF PAUL'S LIFE AND 13 LETTER SCROLLS
- ● UNDERLAY: RED

BACKGROUND

The Holy Spirit continues Jesus' presence beyond his historical life. Paul discovered this on the road to Damascus and elaborated his thinking about what happened in his letters. He knew Jesus in a new way, quite different from the way the disciples knew Jesus. The Holy Spirit draws aside a curtain so we can be "in," "with" and "of" Christ, who has been there all the time, waiting to be found.

This lesson presents the story of Paul's discovering the power of the Holy Spirit. The narrative is important in itself, but it is also one that can be connected to the Creator (see *The Complete Guide to Godly Play, Volume 2,* Lesson 2, pp. 41-48) and Christ (see this volume, Lessons 2-8, pp. 32-68). The Holy Trinity is a synthesis lesson (pp. 136-142) that provides a narrative introduction to the dynamic concept and symbol of the Holy Trinity. This ancient and powerful view of God challenges us to be more sensitive to the complexity of God's elusive presence.

In the beginning of Acts, Luke tells us that just before his ascension, Jesus responded to the disciples' question about the restoration of the kingdom by saying, "It is not for you to know the times or periods that the Father has set by his own authority. But you will receive power when the Holy Spirit has come upon you; and you will be my witnesses in Jerusalem, in all Judea and Samaria, and to the ends of the earth" (Acts 1:7-8). Paul was one of the witnesses who went to the "ends of the earth" in the power of the Holy Spirit.

NOTES ON THE MATERIAL

Find this material on the top shelf of the New Testament shelves of the Sacred Story shelves. A box holds:

- thirteen letter scrolls, one for each of Paul's New Testament letters
- the rolled-up red underlay
- seven wood or foamcore cards with illustrations of the following seven moments in Paul's life:
  1. Leaving Tarsus
  2. Studying at the Temple
  3. Experience on the Road to Damascus
  4. Escape from Damascus
  5. Letters to New Churches
  6. Jerusalem for the Last Time
  7. Paul's Death

The basket also holds a red underlay on which the cards are laid out.

THE SEVEN PAUL CARDS AND THEIR SOURCES

The New Testament story of Paul is found primarily the Acts of the Apostles, which tells the story from Pentecost through Paul's final days in Rome. The narrative begins with Peter, and Paul doesn't appear until the stoning of Stephen in 7:58. From then on, Paul takes over the story. The following seven moments tempt the child to know more:

1. LEAVING TARSUS (PAUL'S BIRTH)

Paul refers to his birth in the speech he made to the angry mob on his last journey to Jerusalem. See Acts 22:3.

2. STUDYING AT THE TEMPLE

In the same speech in Jerusalem, Paul also referred to having been a student of Gamaliel. See Acts 22:3.

3. EXPERIENCE ON THE ROAD TO DAMASCUS (BAPTISM BY THE HOLY SPIRIT)

The story of Paul's encounter with Jesus' presence on the road to Damascus occurs early in Acts (see 9:1-19). He refers to this event twice more, once in his the speech to the angry mob in Jerusalem (Acts 22:6-16) and again during his defense before King Agrippa (26:12-18).

4. ESCAPE FROM DAMASCUS (AND PAUL'S TIME IN THE DESERT)

The escape from Damascus appears in Acts 9:23-25. Paul refers to it in 2 Corinthians 11:32-33 and briefly notes his time in the desert of Arabia in Galatians 1:17.

5. LETTERS TO NEW CHURCHES (PAUL'S WORK: TELLING ABOUT THE POWER OF THE HOLY SPIRIT AND WRITING LETTERS)

Paul's missionary journeys are primarily found in Acts:
- First Journey, Acts 13:1-14, 28
- The Jerusalem Conference, Acts 15:1-35
- Second Journey, Acts 15:36–18:22
- Third Journey, Acts 18:23–21:16

The letters of Paul are not literary, like those of Aristotle, Epicurus or Paul's contemporary Seneca, a Roman who wrote "moral epistles." Nor are they personal, like most of the papyrus letters from the first and second centuries. Paul's letters are somewhere between, meant to be read aloud and passed among congregations. We still follow this tradition when we read and discuss these letters in church.

This lesson uses the New Testament collection of Paul's letters. Not all scholars are convinced that he was the author of all of the thirteen letters that bear his name. The debate over Pauline authorship is not our focus here, but here are the unquestioned and questioned Pauline writings:

Unquestioned	Questioned
1 Thessalonians	2 Thessalonians
Galatians	Colossians
Philippians	Ephesians
Philemon	Titus (pastoral letter)
1 Corinthians	1 Timothy (pastoral letter)
2 Corinthians	2 Timothy (pastoral letter)
Romans	

The questioned writings were probably written by disciples of Paul, who saw themselves as speaking for him and continuing his presence in the Church. For a well-balanced treatment of this issue, please see Chapter 25 of Raymond E. Brown's *An Introduction to the New Testament* (New York: Doubleday, 1997).

6. JERUSALEM FOR THE LAST TIME

Paul's final journey to Jerusalem resulted in his becoming a prisoner of the Romans. He was then moved to the coast, to Caesarea, and finally sailed by ship to Rome by way of Crete and Malta to be tried in the Roman courts, as was his right as a Roman citizen. See Acts 2:17–28:31.

7. PAUL'S DEATH (DEATH AND YET...)

The known chronology of Paul's life begins sometime after Jesus' death about AD 30. If it took about two years for the events of Acts 1–8 to take place, then Paul's conversion happened about AD 32. By AD 60–62, we find him in Rome under house arrest.

Legend takes over where Acts ends. Paul was probably executed in Rome during the rule of Nero, who died by his own hand on June 9, 68. Paul may have lived in Rome during the years between his house arrest and death, or he may have gone to Spain for a time and returned to his death.

As a Roman citizen, Paul was probably executed by the sword or an ax. (Noncitizens were killed by burning, in the games or by crucifixion.) Where did he die? There are two traditions: One is based on the legend that Paul's head bounced three times after it was severed from his body, resulting in three springs that started flowing at each spot where it touched the earth. This place is called, appropriately, *Tre Fontane* ("Three Fountains"). The other tradition holds that the location of his death and burial is the spot where Constantine built a basilica around 324. Today that church is called St. Paul's Outside the Walls. Another tradition links these two sites: One Lucina was said to have carried Paul's remains from *Tre Fontane*, where he was killed, to his burial place at St. Paul's Outside the Walls.

Storytelling Tip: As in the Creation story, you will lay the cards out on a strip, moving from your right to left, so the children can "read" the story being laid out from their left to right.

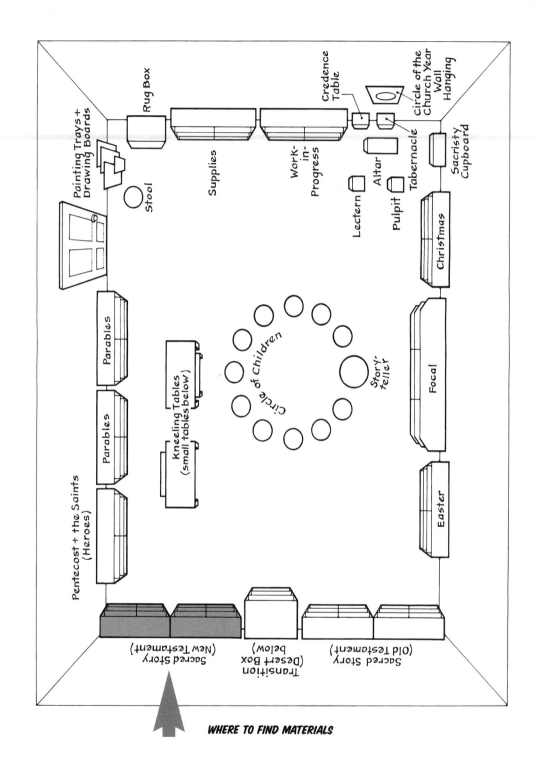

WHERE TO FIND MATERIALS

MOVEMENTS

When the children are settled, go and get the material. Place it beside you. Wait for the children to be ready again, then begin.

LEAVING TARSUS (PAUL'S BIRTH)

Unroll the red underlay far enough to your left so there is a space for the first card.

Place the first card, "Leaving Tarsus," on the underlay, facing the children.

STUDYING AT THE TEMPLE

Unroll the red underlay far enough so there is space for the second card, "Studying at the Temple." Place the card so that it touches the first card.

WORDS

Watch carefully where I go so you will always know where to find this material.

In the beginning the baby was born. His mother and father named him Saul after the first king of Israel. His home was in a city called Tarsus, near the sea.

As the boy grew, he helped his father in his shop. Saul's father made tents. Even though Saul's family lived far from Rome and were Jewish, they were made Roman citizens like many others in the city. Perhaps this had something to do with making tents for the Roman army.

Saul heard many languages in the streets of Tarsus, but it was the language of the synagogue he loved most. His father and he read the Torah together. Saul was very serious about knowing the Hebrew Bible.

Saul grew. When it was time, he decided to go to the great city of Jerusalem, so he could have the best of all the teachers. He waved goodbye to his family and home in Tarsus and traveled to the holy city.

When Saul entered the city through the great high gate, he went first to the Temple. He worshiped there. That is probably also where he studied and worked. His teacher was Gamaliel, or another rabbi in Gamaliel's family. Saul wanted to be one of the Pharisees, who worked hard to keep all of the laws in the Torah.

Saul did work hard to keep the laws. He had no time or patience for people who did not. One day he heard about the Followers of the Way. They thought that the Messiah had come. It was Jesus of Nazareth.

When Saul heard that, he became angry. The Messiah was supposed to drive away the Roman soldiers and rule with justice and mercy. Jesus was a criminal who was crucified. Besides, in the Law it says that God curses any criminal who is "hanged upon a tree." These people were telling lies about God. He had to stop them from saying such things.

MOVEMENTS

WORDS

Stephen was one of the most important of the Followers of the Way. He was tried by the court in the Temple and taken outside the city to be stoned to death.

Saul held the coats of the ones who threw stones at Stephen until he died. Then Saul was given a letter by the High Priest to go to Damascus to catch more Followers of the Way and bring them back to Jerusalem for punishment.

EXPERIENCE ON THE ROAD TO DAMASCUS (BAPTISM BY THE HOLY SPIRIT)

Unroll the red underlay far enough so there is a space for the third card, "Experience on the Road to Damascus." Place the card so that it touches the card in the second position.

Saul traveled to Damascus. On that afternoon he climbed up the road toward the city. Suddenly there was a great light! It was so bright that he fell to the ground. He could see nothing.

In his darkness a voice came to him: "Saul, Saul, why are you trying to hurt me? Why are you persecuting me?"

All Saul could say was, "Who are you, Lord?"

The voice answered, "I am Jesus, the one you are persecuting. Get up. Go into the city. You will be told what to do."

Saul tried to get up. He looked for the path, but he was blind.

Saul was led into the city and left at a house on Straight Street. For three days he went without food or water. Then, in the chaos and the darkness of his blindness, he heard another voice. "Hello, brother Saul, I am Ananias. I was sent by Jesus to lay hands on you and bless you."

When Ananias' hands touched Saul, something like the scales from a fish fell from his eyes and he could see. Then Ananias baptized him. Saul was changed forever. He could feel the power of the Holy Spirit growing inside of him. Then Ananias and Saul ate together.

Slowly Saul regained his strength. When he was better, he went to the synagogue to tell his fellow Jews the good news about what had happened to him. When they heard what Saul said, they tried to kill him. They even put guards at the city gate to catch him if he tried to get away, but Followers of the Way hid Saul in the city and they couldn't find him.

MOVEMENTS	WORDS

ESCAPE FROM DAMASCUS (AND PAUL'S TIME IN THE DESERT)

Unroll the red underlay far enough so there is space for the fourth card, "Escape from Damascus." Place the card so that it touches the third card.

One night when it was dark, Saul and a small group of the Followers of the Way climbed quietly up to the top of the city wall. They carried a large basket and lots of rope. They tied the rope to the basket, and Saul climbed inside. They lowered him down the wall and he disappeared into the dark.

Saul went into the desert of Arabia. He was confused and needed to understand what God wanted him to do. He had come to Damascus to catch Followers of the Way, but now he was one of them. What did this mean?

Saul prayed. He watched the empty desert and listened to its silence. He came so close to God and God came so close to him that he knew what God wanted him to do.

He was to travel to the ends of the earth and tell people what had happened to him, for he had changed. His work was to try to say how his hate had turned into love and to begin churches where people could show how this was done. He also was to write letters to help new churches do this.

LETTERS TO NEW CHURCHES (PAUL'S WORK: TELLING ABOUT THE POWER OF THE HOLY SPIRIT AND WRITING LETTERS)

Unroll the red underlay far enough so there is space for the fifth card.

Saul began his work. He sailed across the sea. He walked across the land.

He went back to Jerusalem to meet with Peter, James and the others there, now called Christians. They were suspicious, but they finally said to keep telling the story to the Gentiles, the non-Jews.

Saul even changed his name. He was traveling so much in the Roman Empire that he began to use his Roman name, "Paul."

Place the fifth card, "Letters to New Churches," so that it touches the fourth card.

Paul's work was to start churches, but he also wrote letters to young churches to help them with their problems. He wrote to the Philippians and the Ephesians. He wrote to the Thessalonians and the Corinthians. He even wrote to the Romans and told them he wanted to visit them and then go on to Spain.

MOVEMENTS

JERUSALEM FOR THE LAST TIME

Unroll the red underlay far enough so there is a space for the sixth card, "Jerusalem for the Last Time." Place the sixth card so that it touches the fifth card.

PAUL'S DEATH (DEATH AND YET...)

Unroll the red underlay far enough so there is a space for the seventh card.

Place the seventh card, "Paul's Death," so that it touches the sixth card.

WORDS

Paul turned toward Jerusalem for the last time. As soon as he came into the city he went to the Temple. He wanted to make a sacrifice. He was still a Nazarite, keeping strict Jewish law, as well as being a Christian.

People shouted that he didn't belong there. Some began to push him. The Roman soldiers came running. They pushed the people back with their shields, short swords and spears. They saved Paul's life and marched him to the Fortress Antonia.

The Roman soldiers decided to beat him to find out why the Jews wanted to kill him, but that was when Paul told them he was a Roman citizen. He had to be taken to the Roman courts.

He was taken to Caesarea on the coast. After about two years he was put on a ship that was sailing to Rome to be judged in the law courts there.

Paul sailed to Rome. His ship sank, but he was saved and went on anyway.

Paul was kept a prisoner in his own house. A soldier guarded him, but he could go visit friends while he was waiting for the Roman court to decide what he had done wrong.

Some say that Paul went on to Spain and then came back to Rome. Others think he was executed after the great fire which burned Rome in the year 67. I like to think of Paul as still traveling on "to the ends of the earth."

MOVEMENTS

WORDS

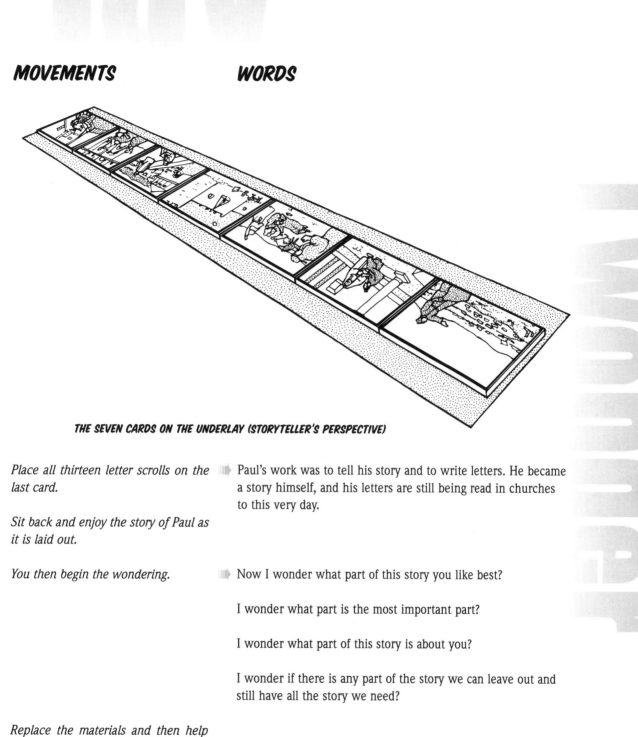

THE SEVEN CARDS ON THE UNDERLAY (STORYTELLER'S PERSPECTIVE)

Place all thirteen letter scrolls on the last card.

Paul's work was to tell his story and to write letters. He became a story himself, and his letters are still being read in churches to this very day.

Sit back and enjoy the story of Paul as it is laid out.

You then begin the wondering.

Now I wonder what part of this story you like best?

I wonder what part is the most important part?

I wonder what part of this story is about you?

I wonder if there is any part of the story we can leave out and still have all the story we need?

Replace the materials and then help the children choose their work.

LESSON 15

THE HOLY TRINITY

FOCUS:
- SACRED STORY
- CORE PRESENTATION

THE MATERIAL
- LOCATION: SACRED STORY SHELVES, EASTER SHELVES, FOCAL SHELVES
- PIECES: CREATION MATERIALS; FACES MATERIALS; PAUL'S DISCOVERY MATERIALS; 3 WHITE CIRCLES FROM BAPTISM MATERIALS (SEE NOTES ON THE MATERIAL, BELOW, FOR FULL LISTINGS)
- UNDERLAY: NONE

BACKGROUND

Through the sacred stories, we have followed God's elusive presence. In the fourth century, the People of God discovered yet another way to understand this experience. It was by a strange three-in-one logic. The stories in which God, Jesus and the Holy Spirit were characters were somehow one story, and yet distinct. This way of thinking preserved the unique aspects of the stories, yet joined them as one.

The Holy Trinity's inner communication is unknown to us. This is because we are created beings, made by God. We can only guess about this inner communication from what we know about how we experience God's relationship with us. As Catherine Mowry LaCugna has powerfully argued in *God for Us* (SanFrancisco: HarperSan-Francisco, 1973), "The doctrine of the Trinity is ultimately therefore a teaching not about the abstract nature of God, nor about God in isolation from everything other than God, but a teaching about God's life with us and our life with each other" (p. 1).

This lesson combines three narratives, transforming them into the concept of the Holy Trinity. That's exactly what happened in the history of the Church in the 4th century. Under the pressure of Greek philosophy, the Church integrated three narratives, like the ones in this lesson, and developed its three-in-one logic to make them one and yet keep them distinct.

NOTES ON THE MATERIAL

The materials for this lesson are three stories told with cards or plaques. Two of the stories are found in this volume: the Faces of Easter (Lessons 2-8, pp. 32-68) and

Paul's Discovery (Lesson 14, pp. 126-135). The third story, Creation, is found in *The Complete Guide to Godly Play, Volume 2* (Lesson 2, pp. 41-48). Each of these three stories is grouped into seven units. as shown here:

Faces of Easter	*Days of Creation*	*Journeys of Paul*
1. Jesus' Birth and Growth	1. Light and Dark	1. Leaving Tarsus (Paul's Birth)
2. Jesus Is Lost and Found	2. Water	2. Studying at the Temple
3. Jesus' Baptism and Blessing by God	3. Dry Land and Growing Things	3. Experience on the Road to Damascus (Baptism by the Holy Spirit)
4. Jesus' Desert and Discovery Experience	4. Day and Night	4. Escape from Damascus (and Paul's Time in the Desert)
5. Jesus as Healer and Parable-Maker	5. Swimming and Flying Creatures	5. Letters to the Churches (Paul's Work: Telling about the Power of the Holy Spirit and Writing Letters)
6. Jesus Offers the Bread and Wine	6. Creatures that Walk	6. Jerusalem for the Last Time
7. The One Who Was Easter and Still Is	7. Rest and Remember	7. Paul's Death (Death and Yet...)

Finally, you will need, from the Holy Baptism lesson (*The Complete Guide to Godly Play, Volume 3,* Lesson 6, pp. 70-76), the three white circles. You will lay these circles, the symbol of the Trinity, over the curious "mess" we have created and begin to wonder about the ways God relates to us, the ways we relate to God, and the ways God relates to God within the communion of the Trinity itself.

SPECIAL NOTES

Storytelling Tip: Because this lesson pulls together three stories through the means of a *fourth* lesson (Holy Baptism), we suggest its use only with older children who are already familiar with the stories of Creation, Holy Baptism, the Faces of Easter and Paul's Discovery. You, too, will need to be familiar with these presentations to tell this synthesis lesson. (See the page citations for each story in the directions above.) The directions given below will tell you only how to adjust the basic presentations for this synthesis lesson.

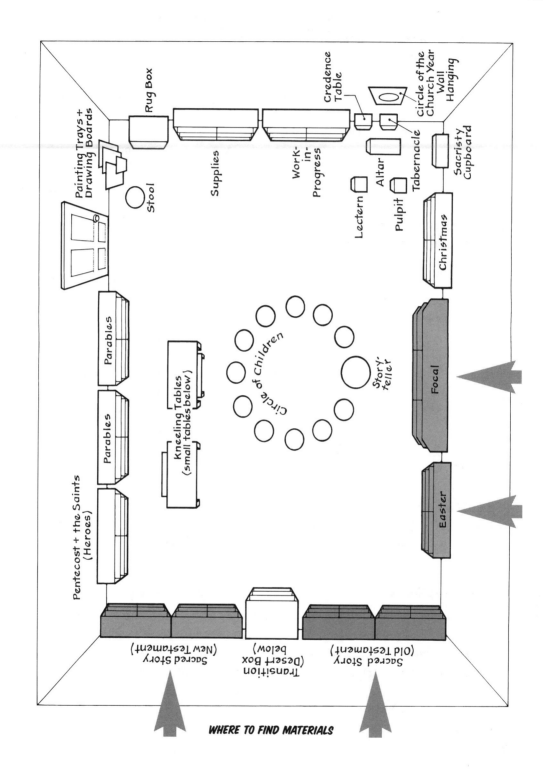

Rug Box

Painting Trays +
Drawing Boards

Supplies

Work-
in-
Progress

Credence
Table

circle of the
Church Year
Wall Hanging

Stool

Lectern

Altar

Pulpit

Tabernacle

Sacristy
Cupboard

Parables

Christmas

Parables

Kneeling Tables
(small tables below)

circle of Children

Story-
teller

Focal

Pentecost + the Saints
(Heroes)

Easter

Sacred Story
(New Testament)

Transition
(Desert Box
below)

Sacred Story
(Old Testament)

WHERE TO FIND MATERIALS

MOVEMENTS

When the children are settled, go and get the materials for the Faces of Easter, Creation, Paul's Discovery and Holy Baptism. Place the materials for two of the presentations on one side of you, and the materials for the other two presentations on the other side of you.

First present the Faces of Easter. Lay it out vertically (see the illustrations on pp. 46, 51, 56, 62 and 66), so the life of Jesus grows away from you toward the children in the circle. Omit the usual wondering questions. Instead, after you present the seventh card, say:

Begin the presentation of Creation. Omit the beginning about the "biggest present you ever got." Instead, merely begin with the first day. When you finish the Creation story, omit the wondering questions. Instead invite the children to combine the two lessons as follows.

Pause a moment. Look at the Creation and the Faces of Easter. Speak slowly and with wonder.

Pick up the first Creation card, that shows "light." Look at it, then look directly at the children.

Don't place the card down without direction from the children. Only if they have no suggestions would you offer an example by picking a place that seems right to you on that day.

As you respond to the children's suggestions, there are several queries you can make, for example:

WORDS

⇒ Watch carefully where I go so you will always know where to find this material.

There's a lot, isn't there.

⇒ You know this lesson. You have seen it before, but there is always more. Now let me show you something interesting.

⇒ Hmm. Look at this.

⇒ I wonder where this day goes in that story.

⇒ Let's try this.

⇒ Shall I put the card here? Should I place it beside or above? Below? Do they need to be touching? Do you want it to also touch this other card? Shall I turn it like this?

MOVEMENTS

Let the children make their own decisions about such questions of placement. Affirm and support the children's choices, including the choice of diverse ideas.

After all the Creation cards are placed with the Face cards, say:

Begin to lay out and tell the Paul's Discovery. Omit the wondering questions at the end.

When the story is finished, sit back. Look back and forth between the story you have just presented and the two stories integrated together.

Pick up the first Paul card.

Again, place the card according to the children's suggestions. Ask questions to clarify their directions.

Finally, you will have guided the placing of all the Paul story with the Faces and with the days of Creation. Sit back again. Look at the clutter.

Turn to the Holy Baptism lesson beside you and pick up the large three white circles. Leave them rolled up for a moment.

Unroll and smooth out each one as you place it over the mixed-up cards. Form three connecting circles that cover as much of the cards as possible. Smooth out each circle as you name it.

Sit back and look at what you have done.

WORDS

Those are all wonderful ideas. I'm just going to place the card here, so we can go on. When you work with this on your own or with a friend, you can put it anywhere you want to.

Now let me show you something else.

I wonder where this card goes in those stories?

I wonder where these cards go in those stories? Hmm. Here is Paul studying in the Temple. Here he is on the Road to Damascus.

Oh, my, what a curious "mess"! What shall we do? It is all mixed up.

This is the Baptism lesson. We don't need all of it. Let's just take these three circles.

When we baptize someone we baptize him or her in "the name of the Father, and of the Son, and of the Holy Spirit."

There, that's better. Now the stories are all connected by the circles, and yet each one is still there by itself. This is a strange kind of three-in-one thinking.

MOVEMENTS	WORDS
Touch one of the circles.	You see? They are all connected and yet each one is still there. It just isn't by itself anymore.
Touch each circle again.	This is a symbol for the Holy Trinity. It is the Father, the Son and the Holy Spirit, one God and yet still three stories about God. We know each story tells something different about God, and yet they are still all together at the same time. That's the three-in-one thinking.
Sit back again.	Now I wonder which one of the three-in-one ways you like best to come close to God?
	I wonder which one of the three-in-one ways is the most important way to come close to God?
	I wonder which one of the three-in-one ways is most like the way you come close to God most easily? Which one is the most natural for you?
	I wonder which one of the three-in-one ways we can leave out and still have all the ways we need?
You can wonder, too, about how God relates to God within the Trinity. This is presumptuous wondering, but many great theologians like St. Thomas Aquinas have wondered about this before us.	I wonder which one of the three-in-one ways God likes best to be with God?
	I wonder which one of the three-in-one ways God knows is the most important way to be with God?
	I wonder which one of the three-in-one ways is the way God most easily and naturally is with God?
	I wonder if God can leave out any of the three-in-one ways to be with God and still have all the ways God needs to be God?
When the wondering loses its energy, you can then begin to put the lesson back into its various trays and baskets. Show all of this putting away to the children so they will not feel as if they have to hurry. It is a lot to put away, but you want to show that you are still involved with all the parts of the synthesis as well as the whole.	Remember you don't have to hurry. Look at all of this. I really do wonder how these stories fit together? I wonder how they are one and yet three? It is easy to see that they are, but it's hard to talk about, isn't it? God is not so simple and yet God is, and that is truly wonderful.

MOVEMENTS

Help the children choose their own work.

WORDS

Remember to be thinking about what work you are going to get out while I am putting all of this away. It's a lot, isn't it? There.

Now, I wonder what work you would like to get out today? It could be about the Trinity, or it could be about something else. Does anyone have unfinished work?

THE PART THAT HASN'T BEEN WRITTEN YET

LESSON NOTES

FOCUS:

- SACRED STORY
- ENRICHMENT PRESENTATION

THE MATERIAL

- LOCATION: SACRED STORY (NEW TESTAMENT) SHELVES
- PIECES: BOOK STAND, BLANK BOOK
- UNDERLAY: NONE

BACKGROUND

The journey with the elusive presence of God will continue. We are not sure what will happen. The future is the time of the children.

NOTES ON THE MATERIAL

Find this material on the far right of the top shelf of the New Testament Sacred Story shelves.

The material is a blank book or journal on a book stand. Find or buy a journal and stand that are beautiful, mysterious and intriguing. You do not plan a time for this presentation. You wait until children ask you about the material before offering this presentation.

SPECIAL NOTES

Storytelling Tip: Your favorite book store is a good source for beautiful blank journals, or you can visit this website:

- *www.levenger.com*

Another possibility would be to borrow a book from the library on making books and to create your own journal.

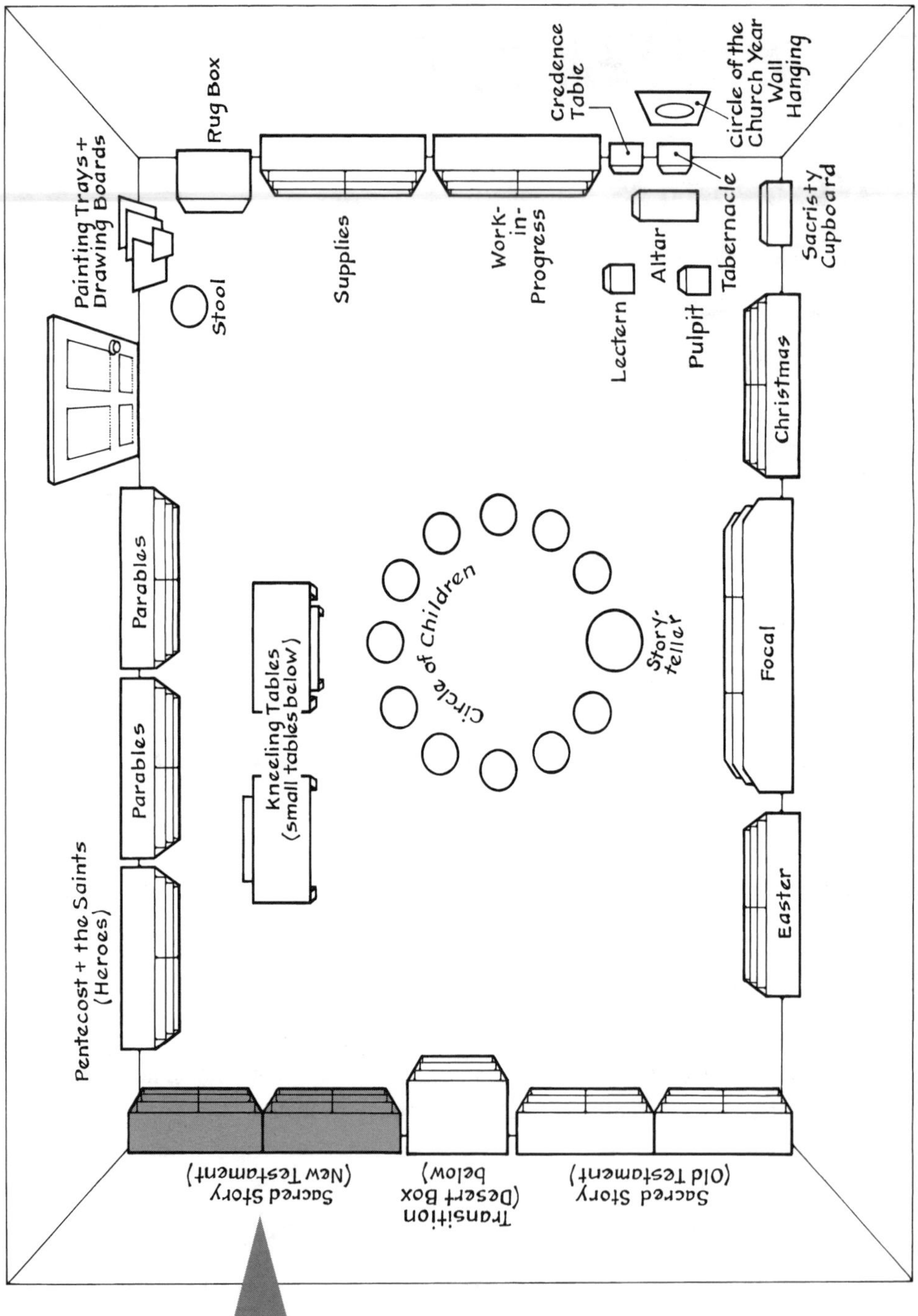
Rug Box
Painting Trays + Drawing Boards
Stool
Supplies
Work-in-Progress
Credence Table
Circle of the Church Year Wall Hanging
Tabernacle
Altar
Lectern
Pulpit
Sacristy Cupboard
Christmas
Focal
Easter
Story-teller
Circle of Children
Kneeling Tables (small tables below)
Parables
Parables
Pentecost + the Saints (Heroes)
Sacred Story (New Testament)
Transition (Desert Box below)
Sacred Story (Old Testament)

WHERE TO FIND MATERIALS

MOVEMENTS

This presentation begins when a child or a group of children come to you to ask about this strange material, i.e., the book stand and book. They might ask, "What is this for?"

Now you can respond. The italicized questions that follow in this column of movement directions are questions that the children might ask—or that you might suggest yourself.

Who will write it?

What will we do?

WORDS

➡ This is the part that hasn't been written yet.

➡ You will. I will not be there.

➡ I don't know. That is up to you. What *will* you do? What will you write in the book about the journey of the People of God with the elusive presence of God?

You may write something now or wait until later. When you are finished, remember to put the material back.